LES LÉGUMES

PASCALE BEALE

LES LÉGUMES

Vegetable Recipes from the Market Table

Foreword by

CAT CORA

Published by

M27 Editions LLC
3030 State Street
Santa Barbara, California 93105
PHONE (805) 563-0099
FAX (805) 563-2070
EMAIL publish@m27editions.com
WEB www.m27editions.com

For cooking classes and merchandise:
WEB www.pascaleskitchen.com
EMAIL info@pascaleskitchen.com

Les Légumes: Vegetable Recipes from the Market Table
by Pascale Beale

Copyright 2017 by Pascale Beale and M27 Editions
Foreword Copyright 2017 by Cat Cora

First Printing

ISBN: 978-0-9968635-1-3
Library of Congress Catalog Number: 2017902155

Design, Photography and Production by Media 27, Inc.

WWW.MEDIA27.COM

Printed in China

For my grandmother Geneviève

Who showed me the way

Contents

Foreword

I GREW UP ON A STEADY DIET OF fusion food long before it became trendy—a multi-cultural mix of Greek cuisine and Southern cooking—eating everything from classic *horiatiki*, *spanakopita* and *kota kapama,* to grits with feta and southern style greens finished with Greek olive oil. My family believed in cooking food from scratch, cooking with the seasons using the best locally available fruits and vegetables, and flavoring everything with a liberal dose of the herbs, spices, garlic and condiments that reflected their respective ethnic upbringings. They believed, as I do, that the preparing and sharing of food has the ability to connect people in a way that few other things can.

It is through good food that I met Pascale. The occasion was judging a local "Iron Chef" type of competition in the town we both call home. Over the years that followed, our paths crisscrossed through an assortment of culinary events, and we realized that we not only share European roots and a multi-cultural upbringing, but also a love of Provence and Mediterranean food, and a similar food philosophy—that of letting the ingredients speak for themselves in uncomplicated cooking.

During a winery tour and luncheon for food bloggers and writers in the Santa Ynez Valley in California, I was able to truly savor Pascale's food. For the event, she had prepared sweet and savory pluot and goat cheese crostini, caramelized onion and olive tapenade tarts, a melt-in-your-mouth slow roasted salmon with a fragrant black rice and a fresh fig relish, and a trio of delectable desserts including an ethereal Eton Mess—all dishes from her just-then released cookbook, *Les Fruits*. Her food embraced the ingredients, and was packed with fresh herbs and bright flavors that truly reflect her penchant for Mediterranean food.

When Pascale asked me if I would write the foreword for *Les Légumes*, the third in her Market Table series, I said yes, of course!

Les Légumes is a book that celebrates vegetables. The twelve, beautifully photographed, ingredient-driven chapters are feature flavor-filled, innovative combinations that showcase a multitude of cuisines from sun-drenched California to the rim of the Mediterranean Sea. Among the more than 100 dishes: a fragrant play on the traditional pissaladiere we tasted at the winery (page 147), a lemon-infused spring leek and pea salad with burrata (page 136), a light, herb-filled, frothy zucchini cappuccino (page 228), her whimsical tasty take on mushrooms growing in the wild (page 156), and an "accordion" of tomatoes and eggplant suffused with aromatic *herbes de Provence* (page 104).

In this book, Pascale has embraced plant-based cooking and takes her readers far beyond the preparation of plain steamed vegetables. Accompanied by engaging anecdotes, her recipes are filled with an abundance of herbs and infused with fruity olive oils. The vegetables are grilled, roasted, sautéed, braised and raw, and Pascale offers a delicious array of vegetable-focused dishes from simple appetizers, wildly colorful salads and superb soups, to magnificent curries, tagines, tourtes and tarts.

Les Légumes is not only a feast for the eyes, it will also delight your taste buds.

> *Kali orexi! Bon appétit!*
> *Cat Cora*

Cat Cora made television history in 2005 when she became the first female Iron Chef on Food Network's Iron Chef America. Since then, she's become a prominent figure in the culinary community, first woman to be inducted into the Culinary Hall of Fame, and beyond as an accomplished author, restaurateur, contributing editor, television host, avid philanthropist, lifestyle entrepreneur, and proud mother of six.

Introduction

GROWING UP IN England and France, I ate a fairly classic diet of meat or fish and two vegetables, albeit with some Indian-Chinese-North African-Provençal elements thrown in. Now living in California, I am drawn inexorably toward a more fruit- and vegetable-centric Mediterranean-style diet. While I am not vegetarian, vegetables have become a central part of all my meals. I am inspired, in large part, by the food I find at my local farmers markets. I love the seasonal, colorful variety and assorted flavors and textures that vegetables provide; I appreciate their versatility, as well as their health benefits.

I grew up learning about vegetables, first by helping in the kitchen. My earliest memory of preparing food is tied to vegetables—grating carrots to be specific. I was no more than five years old, sitting on my favorite red stool in my grandmother Genevieve's kitchen. She made a fabulous salad with those grated carrots—to this day, a favorite dish of my mine and my brother's.

I continued to learn by shopping for produce with my mother and grandmother in France. The basis of good cooking, they said, was to select ingredients at their peak. I learnt about cooking with and through the seasons, and to relish vegetables in their prime. My mother and grandmother taught me, for example, to look for firm, glossy eggplants; to avoid potatoes that had begun to sprout; to choose carrots with a bright snap; to examine the leaves of leafy topped vegetables to make sure they were bright green; and to gently squeeze endives to make sure they were firm. *Il faut toujours bien regarder, sentir, et si possible de gouter avant de choisir.* "It is always necessary to examine, to smell, and, if possible, to taste before choosing," they would say.

My favorite days, wherever I find myself in the world, be it California, London or Provence—the places I call home—are market days. I eagerly anticipate them. I love to meander from stall to stall, to linger, to smell, to taste, to soak up the atmosphere unique to each locale, to chat with friends, talk with farmers about their latest harvest and strike up conversations with passersby. Season after season, these farmers markets stir my creative juices and literally nourish me, body and soul. My rhythms of the seasons are punctuated by my visits to the farmers market.

For some, winter markets seem tedious, an uninteresting parade of little more than Brussels sprouts, potatoes and onions. While those vegetables are certainly abundant during this season, there are so many more fantastic choices, such as vibrant winter greens, watercress and rainbow-colored chard, and so many creative ways to transform even the stodgiest of dishes. I also love the fruits of the season—blood oranges, persimmons, pomegranates and Meyer lemons—and how they enhance the vibrant color and freshness of rich carrot purées, brighten a roasted acorn squash salad, or transform a simple cauliflower into a curried soup piled high with lemon-scented crispy shaved Brussels sprouts. I love how they perfume, enliven and complement winter vegetables and bring a tangy freshness to otherwise traditional cold-weather comfort foods.

After a long cool winter, I often crave not only some warm sunshine—yes, even in California—but spring vegetables with their crisp, bright, herbaceous flavors. I have always felt as though, after months of hibernation, the earth has awakened and decided to shower us with a multitude of delicacies, each one fresh, invigorating and tempting, prompting a type of visceral spring fever.

I admit I tend to go a little overboard at the market when I spy the first of the season's small purple artichokes and freshly picked spring asparagus; that I will go plunging into a pyramid of peas, or lust after luminescent fava beans and pea sprouts; that I will gather up baby zucchini with bright yellow flowers by the basketful; and pick an abundance of fresh herbs and bouquets of basil—lemon-scented, Thai and purple. Is there anything better than filling your market basket with these eye-popping vegetables, then coming home, preparing them, and cooking them in a multitude of ways or simply drizzling them with a fruity olive oil and a pinch of coarse sea salt?

Just when I think the markets cannot get any better, summer vegetables come bursting to life, and the farmers market tables groan under the weight of magnificent heirloom tomatoes, plump purple eggplants, colorful whimsical pattypan squash, multi-hued haricots verts and sun-drenched corn. It's food that makes me want to dine outside, to have barbecues, picnics and languorous afternoons on the grass while eating bowls of bright salads and grilled vegetables accompanied by a cool tzatziki, some freshly baked bread and delectable cheese.

Then, as the days grow shorter and a chill creeps into the air, my thoughts turn naturally to the autumnal dishes that comfort me. It's time for big bowls of soup made from

sculptural squashes, and roasts with masses of the root vegetables I find piled higgledy-piggledy on market tables. It's a time for risottos with wild mushrooms and spiced tagines with parsnips, pumpkins, onions and multi-colored carrots. I always think of the autumn as a time of gathering—a bringing together of family and friends, a harvest of sorts, a reaping not only of autumnal crops, but of the year's hard work before we settle in for the winter months.

Now, whenever I shop, whatever the time of year, I can hear my grandmother's voice guiding my hand to choose a particular head of lettuce, a firm cauliflower or radiant bunch of radishes. I remember *"regarder, sentir, et si possible de gouter"* and am inspired to create new dishes as the ingredients come together in my basket in an ever-changing kaleidoscope of beautiful and delicious vegetables. I hope *Les Légumes* inspires you to do the same.

Bon Appetit!

ASPARAGUS

Asparagus Crostini
with Chanterelles and
Herbed Ricotta

—

Asparagus Wraps

—

Prosciutto-Wrapped
Grilled Asparagus

—

Spring Asparagus and
English Pea Soup

—

Roasted Asparagus with
Buffalo Mozzarella
and Herb-Nut Crunch

—

Shaved Asparagus,
Broccolini and Farro
Salad

—

Grilled Vegetable Salad

—

White and Green
Asparagus Tart

—

Asparagus with
Poached Lemon
Tarragon Chicken

Asparagus Crostini with Chanterelles and Herbed Ricotta

These little toasts are among my favorite springtime nibbles. If I can find fresh chanterelles, and the weather is warm enough to dine *al fresco*, this is the appetizer I make to celebrate the arrival of spring and the start of Sunday lunches in the garden. Asparagus and chanterelle mushrooms are a match made in heaven — the fresh, grass-like quality of one, pairing well with the rustic, earthy qualities of the other. I like to serve the *crostini* with a glass of bubbly or a crisp white wine.

Serves 8 people

For the herbed ricotta:

1 teaspoon olive oil

Zest of 1 lemon

1/2 lb ricotta cheese

1 teaspoon lemon thyme leaves—chopped

1 tablespoon finely chopped chives

For the mushrooms and asparagus:

Olive oil

1 lb thin asparagus—cut on a bias in 1/2-inch pieces, leaving the tips whole

Coarse sea salt

Black pepper

3 tablespoons butter

1 lb chanterelle mushrooms —carefully cleaned and sliced

8 large slices olive bread— toasted

1 Place all the ricotta ingredients in a small bowl, and using a fork, mix together well.

2 Heat a little olive oil in a large skillet. Add the asparagus, a pinch of salt and pepper, and sauté, stirring frequently for 3–4 minutes. Place the asparagus in a bowl.

3 Melt the butter in the same skillet. Add the mushrooms, and cook until they just begin to render their juice, approximately 4–5 minutes. Return the asparagus to the skillet and cook 1–2 minutes more.

4 To assemble the crostini, drizzle the toasts with a little olive oil. Spread with the ricotta mixture and spoon some of the asparagus-mushroom mixture on the top. Serve warm.

Asparagus Wraps

My son, Alexandre, is partial to an afternoon snack of grilled flour tortillas slathered with butter. The aroma of grilling tortillas is seductive. Feeling peckish one day, I made one of my own and decided to fill it with some salad greens, feta and leftover cooked vegetables for a quick, delicious and healthy light lunch. Since then, I have made many variations, including this one with asparagus spears. You can also use grilled zucchini, haricots verts and onions in the filling, substitute a creamy goat cheese for the tangy feta, and add sun-dried tomatoes or avocado slices to the wraps.

Serves 8 people

Olive oil

2 lbs asparagus—
   woody ends removed

Salt

Black pepper

8 eight-inch flour tortillas

1/2 cup Greek yogurt

2 tablespoons finely
   chopped chives

1 small cucumber—peeled,
   sliced lengthwise into
   long 1/4 x 1/4-inch sticks

1/3 cup cilantro leaves—
   roughly chopped

2 oz feta cheese—crumbled

1 Pour a little olive oil into a large skillet over medium-high heat. Add the asparagus, a pinch of salt and 4–5 grinds of pepper. Cook the stalks, stirring gently, for 5–6 minutes. The asparagus should be *al dente* and lightly golden brown.

2 Lightly brown each tortilla directly on the grate of a gas burner over a low-flame, approximately 30–40 seconds. Carefully flip the tortilla and brown the second side, about 20–30 seconds. Watch closely, as tortillas can burn easily. You can also use a grill pan to brown the tortillas, about 30 seconds more per side. Keep the warmed tortillas wrapped in a clean tea towel until ready to use.

3 To assemble the wraps, spread some of the Greek yogurt onto each tortilla and sprinkle with chives. Place the cucumber sticks and grilled asparagus on top. Add the crumbled feta and chopped cilantro. Fold the bottom third of the tortilla over the filling, and then fold in the sides. Serve immediately.

Prosciutto-Wrapped Grilled Asparagus

My grandparents lived in a small French town, only 10 kilometers from the Italian border. When I was a little girl, finding good prosciutto involved driving up an alpine pass and doing a little shopping in the nearest village on the Italian side. We would buy grissini (long thin bread sticks), carefully spread a little salted butter down one side of a single stick, and then wrap it in prosciutto. We were only allowed one each lest it ruin our appetite for dinner. My brother and I would covet our heavenly treats and would try to make them last all the way back to our grandparent's house. We failed every time. Those alpine drives inspired this appetizer. But instead of the grissini, it's asparagus spears; and instead of butter, I use goat cheese. Both versions are delectable and I still have trouble eating only one!

Serves 8 people

16 asparagus spears

Olive oil

Salt

Black pepper

3 oz soft goat cheese

1 tablespoon finely
    chopped chives

1 tablespoon finely
    chopped basil

1 tablespoon lemon juice

16 slices prosciutto

1 Place the asparagus in a shallow dish and drizzle lightly with a little extra virgin olive oil, a pinch of salt and some pepper.

2 Heat a cast iron skillet or grill pan until sizzling hot. Cook the asparagus spears for 3–4 minutes. Turn the spears and grill another 1–2 minutes. Place the asparagus on a plate.

3 In a small bowl, mix together the goat cheese, chives, basil, lemon juice and 5–6 grinds of pepper.

4 Place the prosciutto slices on a clean work surface. Spread the goat cheese mixture over the sliced prosciutto. Wrap each slice of prosciutto around a grilled asparagus stalk. Serve at room temperature.

Spring Asparagus and English Pea Soup

Sweet, tender, bright green asparagus and crisp, fresh, pop-in-your-mouth English peas at the farmers market are tell-tale signs that spring has arrived in full force. When I find both at the market on the same day, I make this soup. Its color is vibrant and the flavor is herbaceous and fresh. A bowl of this with a chunky slice of hearty bread is all I need for dinner.

Serves 8 people

Olive oil

3–4 shallots—finely diced

1½ lbs asparagus—
   stalks thinly sliced

1½ lbs shelled English peas

Coarse sea salt

Black pepper

5 cups vegetable stock

1 Pour a little olive oil into a large saucepan over medium-high heat. Cook the shallots, stirring frequently until lightly golden and fragrant, about 3–4 minutes.

2 Add the asparagus and cook for 2 minutes.

3 Stir in the peas, a good pinch of sea salt, 6–7 grinds of pepper, and cook for 1–2 minutes.

4 Add the vegetable stock and cook for 5–6 minutes over medium-high heat.

5 Using a traditional or immersion blender, purée the soup until completely smooth.

6 Serve hot, with some crusty bread alongside.

Roasted Asparagus with Buffalo Mozzarella and Herb-Nut Crunch

Many years ago, while travelling in Venice, I visited a small, side street restaurant. The trattoria had been highly recommended and I'll admit that when I finally found it—who doesn't get lost in the labyrinth that is Venice—I was a little taken aback by the disheveled look of the place. I entered hesitantly and soon found myself seated at a slightly wobbly, battered wooden table. The owner suggested I order the Caprese salad to start. I was looking for something a little more adventurous and was about to say so when he asked, in his sing-song voice, if I had ever tasted fresh buffalo mozzarella. "No? I bring it to you," he said. End of discussion. He arrived a few minutes later with a plate displaying one sliced tomato, next to which sat one plump mozzarella ball. Nothing else. He waited with arms folded across his chest, nodding encouragingly for me to try it. I don't particularly like being stared at when I eat, but he was not going anywhere until I tasted the mozzarella. I cut into the soft white cheese and took a bite. I may have gasped. The ultra-fresh cheese which had been made less than 24 hours earlier, had a voluptuous texture, akin to silken cream flavored with a hint of herbs. The owner smiled knowingly. Satisfied, he walked away and left me to relish the simple, yet ethereal cheese before me.

Now, whenever I find good buffalo mozzarella, I am reminded of that ethereal cheese in Venice. In this recipe, the soft texture of the cheese contrasts well with the crispness of the asparagus and the crunch from the nuts.

Serves 8 people

2 lbs asparagus—
   woody ends removed

Olive oil

Salt

Black pepper

1 buffalo mozzarella—sliced

1/3 cup raw almonds—
   chopped

2 tablespoons finely
   chopped chives

1 tablespoon finely chopped
   parsley

1 tablespoon finely chopped
   lemon basil

1 tablespoon Dijon mustard

1 tablespoon red wine
   vinegar or fig balsamic
   vinegar

1/4 cup olive oil

1 Preheat the oven to 400 degrees.

2 Place the asparagus stalks onto a rimmed sheet pan. Drizzle with olive oil, a good pinch of salt and 4–5 grinds of pepper. Shake the pan back and forth to evenly coat the stalks. Roast the asparagus for 15-18 minutes or until they are *al dente*, lightly golden on the outside and juicy on the inside. Fan out the cooked asparagus on a large serving platter.

3 Place the sliced mozzarella on top of the cooked asparagus.

4 In a small bowl, mix together the almonds, chives, parsley, and lemon basil. Sprinkle the mixture over the asparagus and mozzarella.

5 In a separate small bowl, whisk together the mustard, olive oil and vinegar to form a thick emulsion. Drizzle the vinaigrette over the asparagus and mozzarella. Serve warm.

Shaved Asparagus, Broccolini and Farro Salad

I developed a taste for raw asparagus when my friend Lynn plucked a spear from its bed as we strolled through her abundant garden. "Try this," she said. An explosion of flavor flooded my taste buds. I wanted to recreate that sensation and found that shaving asparagus results in a similar raw-grassy-herbal flavor. Add the shavings to any grain, such as the farro used in this dish, and you have the makings of a great salad. Farro, with its slightly chewy texture and nutty flavor, beautifully complements the light, fresh asparagus.

Serves 8 people

1¹/₂ cups farro—well rinsed

Olive oil

¹/₂ lb baby broccolini—
   sliced vertically

Salt

Black pepper

Zest and juice of 1 lemon

1 lb asparagus (thick stalks)
   —shaved with a vegetable
   peeler into thin strips

1 bunch watercress—
   tough stems trimmed

¹/₂ cup almonds—
   finely chopped

3 oz Parmesan cheese—
   shaved into thin slices

1 Bring a large saucepan of salted water to a boil. Add the farro and cook until *al dente*, and slightly chewy in texture, about 15–25 minutes. The best way to check for doneness is to taste! Drain the farro, fluff with a fork and let cool in a bowl, or spread out on a rimmed sheet pan.

2 Pour a little olive oil into a medium skillet over medium heat. Add the broccolini, a pinch of salt and 4–5 grinds of pepper, and cook for 2–3 minutes or until just softened.

3 In a large salad bowl, whisk together ¹/₄ cup extra virgin olive oil, the lemon zest and juice, a good pinch of salt and 6–7 grinds of pepper to form an emulsion. Place salad servers over the vinaigrette.

4 Add the cooked farro, broccolini, shaved asparagus, watercress and almonds to the bowl, placing everything on top of the utensils. When ready to serve, toss well to combine. Top with the shaved Parmesan. Serve warm.

NOTE: A lovely, heartier variation of this salad is to add a poached egg onto each person's salad. The egg is delicious when mixed in with the vegetables and farro.

Grilled Vegetable Salad

This salad was inspired by my long-ago visits to The Ivy restaurant when I first came to Los Angeles. Packed with grilled vegetables, it has abundant flavors and a hearty vinaigrette. This is one of my favorite lunchtime dishes.

Serves 8 people

For the vinaigrette:

1 heaped tablespoon Dijon mustard

1/3 cup olive oil

1 tablespoon red wine vinegar or fig balsamic vinegar

Pinch of salt

4–5 grinds black pepper

For the salad:

Olive oil

4 ears of corn— husks removed

Salt

Black pepper

4 medium zucchini—cut on a bias into 1/4-inch slices

8 green onions— ends trimmed

2 lbs asparagus— woody ends removed, stalks left whole

2 tablespoons finely chopped chives

2 tablespoons cilantro leaves

2 tablespoons chopped parsley

3 oz mache (lamb's lettuce)

8 edible flowers such as nasturtiums or pansies (optional)

1 In a large salad bowl, whisk together the vinaigrette ingredients to form a thick emulsion. Place salad utensils over the vinaigrette.

2 Heat a grill pan over medium-high heat. Place the corn on a plate and drizzle with a little olive oil, a pinch of salt and some pepper. Grill, turning the corn every 3 minutes or so, until golden brown on all sides. Place the cooked corn on a cutting board, cut the kernels off the cobs and add them to the salad bowl.

3 Place the sliced zucchini in a medium bowl, drizzle with olive oil and add a pinch of salt and some pepper. Toss to coat.

4 Grill the zucchini slices until they are just cooked, about 2 minutes per side. You may need to do this in batches in order to fit the slices in a single layer. Add the grilled zucchini to the salad bowl.

5 Place the green onions and asparagus on a large plate. Drizzle with a little olive oil and sprinkle with a good pinch of salt and some pepper. Grill over medium-high heat for 3–4 minutes, turn, and cook until lightly charred, about 1–2 minutes. Remove the cooked spears and onions from the pan, cut them into 2-inch pieces and add them to the salad bowl.

6 Add the remaining ingredients except the flowers to the salad bowl and toss well to combine. Divide the salad among eight dinner plates, place a flower in the center of each plate and serve warm.

White and Green Asparagus Tart

There is something quite magical about watching puff pastry rise while it's baking, expanding its buttery layers upon buttery layers. Almost anything added to this tart base tastes incredible. Here I've combined soft, golden brown onions, *al dente* asparagus and a little feta to create a lovely spring tart. I like to serve this with a fresh green salad that's packed with herbs.

Serves 8 people

Olive oil

4 red onions—peeled, halved and thinly sliced

Salt

Black pepper

1 lb white asparagus—ends trimmed and stalks peeled

1 lb green asparagus—ends trimmed

1 rectangular sheet puff pastry—thawed

1 tablespoon finely chopped chives

1 oz feta cheese—crumbled

1 Preheat the oven to 400 degrees.

2 Heat a little olive oil in a medium saucepan. Add the onions, a good pinch of salt and 7–8 grinds of pepper and cook, stirring frequently, until soft and lightly golden, approximately 7–8 minutes. Remove from the heat.

3 Steam the asparagus for 6 minutes. They should be *al dente*. The white variety tend to take a little longer than the green, but they will continue to cook in the oven, so don't worry if they are a little firm at this stage. Remove from the steamer and let cool.

4 Unfold the puff pastry and place it on a parchment lined baking pan. Bake in the center of the oven for 12–14 minutes. The pastry will puff up and turn lightly golden in color. Remove from the oven,

5 Spread the cooked onions over the partially cooked puff pastry to within 1/2 inch of the edge. Arrange the asparagus in alternating colors on top of the onions. Return the tart to the oven and bake for 10–12 minutes or until the pastry is a golden brown.

6 Remove the cooked tart from the oven, immediately sprinkle the chives, and dot with the feta. Serve hot.

Asparagus with Poached Lemon Tarragon Chicken

This dish is a play on the classic French dish *poulet a l'estragon*, a roast chicken scented with the floral and anise-tasting tarragon. Mine is a lighter, more delicate version that uses that same flavor profile. This is a quick dish to prepare, so it's easy to make any night of the week, yet also elegant enough for a special dinner party.

Serves 8 people

1 lb white asparagus—
    ends trimmed, cut on a
    bias into 2-inch pieces,
    leaving the tips whole

1 lb green asparagus—
    ends trimmed, cut on a
    bias into 2-inch pieces,
    leaving the tips whole

Olive oil

3 shallots—peeled
    and thinly sliced

Salt

Black pepper

5–6 sprigs tarragon leaves

3 cups vegetable stock

1/2 lb boneless, skinless
    chicken breasts—
    cut into thin pieces

3 tablespoons crème fraîche

2 tablespoons Dijon or
    tarragon mustard

2 tablespoons finely
    chopped chives

1 Steam the asparagus until just tender, 5 minutes or so. Remove from the steamer.

2 Pour a little olive oil into a large saucepan over medium heat. Add the shallots, a good pinch of salt and 7–8 grinds of pepper, and sauté until just golden, about 3–5 minutes. Stir in the tarragon leaves. Add the vegetable stock and cook for 2 minutes.

3 Poach the chicken in the stock for 6–8 minutes, turning the pieces frequently. Stir in the crème fraîche and mustard and simmer for 1–2 minutes.

4 Add the asparagus and chives, and warm through. Serve in deep plates or shallow bowls with plenty of the cooking liquid. A chunk of crusty bread is delicious alongside to mop up all those aromatic juices.

BEETS & RADISHES

Radishes with Salt,
Butter and Baguettes

—

Radish, Olive and
Watercress Salad

—

Raw Red Beet Salad
with Pomegranates and
Herb-Nut Gremolata

—

Sautéed Radish, Cucumber
and Apple Salad

—

Roasted Baby Beets
with Blood Oranges

—

Daikon, Watermelon
Radish and Beets with
Nut Mustard Vinaigrette

—

Salt Roasted Beets with
Mackerel and Spiced
Onions

—

Roasted Beets and
Butternut Squash with
Zesty Parsley Pesto

Chioggia Beets with Salmon,
Dill, and Crème Fraîche

Radishes with Salt, Butter and Baguettes

If ever there was a dish that epitomized my family's picnics, be they barbecues in my grandparents' garden or on an alpine hike, this is it. No cooking is involved. All you need is a good, fresh baguette, some excellent butter, coarse sea salt and fresh, crisp radishes. Ours is certainly not the first, nor the last family to feature this simple appetizer in our roster of picnic dishes or as an appetizer for dinner parties. It's a perennial favorite all over France. We always come back to it because it is so satisfying. It's the pepperiness of the radishes mingling with the creaminess of the butter, the crunch of the fresh baguette, and the sprinkling of salt that enlivens everything. Dip the radish in the salt, munch, and then have a bite of the buttered baguette. *Délicieux!*

Serves 8 people

1 or 2 bunches breakfast radishes—thoroughly rinsed, ends trimmed

Butter

1 baguette—sliced

Coarse sea salt

1 To serve this as an appetizer, place the radishes in a small bowl or arrange on a serving board with the sliced baguette, fresh butter and a small bowl of salt for dipping the radishes.

Radish, Olive and Watercress Salad with Lemon Yogurt Vinaigrette

This might sound like an odd combination—radishes with olives—but it works. I had made a radish and watercress salad many times before, and decided that now it needed a little *je ne sais quoi* to enliven it. That's when I hit on the idea of adding olives. The saltiness and texture of the olives and lemony yogurt vinaigrette, paired with the pepperiness of the radishes, gave the salad just the pop it needed. I like to serve this with some warm focaccia or crusty bread. You can make a nice variation of the dish by adding feta.

Serves 8 people

For the vinaigrette:

2 tablespoons yogurt

1 tablespoon olive oil

Zest and juice of 1 Meyer
   lemon

Pinch of sea salt

For the salad:

2 bunches radishes—
   ends trimmed,
   very thinly sliced

3 bunches watercress—
   tough stems trimmed

1 cup parsley leaves—
   chopped

1 cup mixed olives—
   pitted and chopped

1/2 cup cilantro leaves

1 Whisk all the vinaigrette ingredients together in a medium salad bowl. Place salad utensils over the vinaigrette.

2 Place all of the salad ingredients in the salad bowl on top of the utensils. When ready to serve, toss together well.

Raw Red Beet Salad with Pomegranates and Herb-Nut Gremolata

My appreciation of beets has come a long way since the boiled-to-death, ice cold, slimy salads that were inflicted on me as an English schoolchild. I would do everything possible to avoid eating them. Now, I will regularly choose salads if I see they have beets in them. This change of heart (and palate) took place after I had moved to California and I first tasted roasted beets. They were juicy, packed with sweet flavor and had a perfect texture. Raw beets are a revelation in their beetiness. (I know that's not a word, but it should be.) Their intense flavor bursts in your mouth. Add the pop of pomegranate and the freshness of herbs, and you have a dish that will make you feel good, vibrant and healthy as soon as you take your first mouthful. That is how I felt after eating this salad for the first time, and how I've felt every time since. I hope you do, too.

Serves 8 people

4 red beets—peeled,
   very thinly sliced on
   a mandolin

Seeds of 1 pomegranate

3 tablespoons olive oil

¼ cup almonds—chopped

1 large shallot—peeled
   and very thinly sliced

Zest and juice of 1 lemon

1 tablespoon balsamic
   vinegar

2 tablespoons finely
   chopped parsley

2 tablespoons finely
   chopped chives

2 tablespoons cilantro leaves

1 Arrange the sliced beets in an attractive pattern on a large serving platter or shallow dish. Scatter the pomegranate seeds on top.

2 In a small bowl, whisk together the olive oil, almonds, shallot, lemon zest and juice and vinegar. Mix in the chopped chives and parsley. Pour the vinaigrette over the beets and let rest at least 30 minutes for the flavors to meld. Sprinkle with cilantro leaves just before serving.

Sautéed Radish, Cucumber and Apple Salad

I think I may have gotten a little carried away when I first shopped for this salad. I had found watermelon radishes at the market and, as I love eating them with apples, planned to make a dish with simply those two ingredients. However, I came across the radish sprouts and then all the other ingredients kept finding their way into my basket, and subsequently into my salad bowl. I love this salad's crunchiness. You can make countless variations by changing the type of nuts used—almonds and pistachios work well—and adding celery and fennel. It's a very refreshing main course for lunch.

Serves 8 people

For the vinaigrette:

1 tablespoon walnut mustard

3 tablespoons olive oil

Juice and zest of 1 lemon

For the salad:

Olive oil

1 bunch assorted small radishes—trimmed, quartered lengthwise

1 watermelon radish—trimmed, peeled and thinly sliced

1/3 cup pecans—chopped

1 cucumber—peeled, quartered lengthwise and sliced

1 large apple—quartered, cored and sliced

Pinch of coarse sea salt

2 tablespoons finely chopped chives

3 tablespoons mint leaves

3 oz feta cheese—crumbled

1 oz radish sprouts

1 In a medium salad bowl, whisk together the vinaigrette ingredients to form a thick emulsion. Place salad utensils over the vinaigrette.

2 Pour a little olive oil into a large skillet over medium-high heat. Add the radishes, pecans and a pinch of salt. Sauté until just golden brown, about 3–4 minutes. Add to the salad bowl.

3 Add all the remaining ingredients to the bowl. When ready to serve, toss well to combine.

Roasted Baby Beets with Blood Oranges and Chive Vinaigrette

Roasting golden beets in their skin preserves their color. When you peel them, it is as though you are unwrapping little tasty golden orbs whose flavor is slightly earthy, yet retains an element of sweetness from the natural sugars in the beets. Combined with the juicy and succulent blood oranges, the beets make this salad is a visual and delectable treat.

Serves 8 people

For the beets and oranges:

3 large yellow beets—
   unpeeled

Olive oil

Salt

4 blood oranges—peeled,
   sliced horizontally

For the vinaigrette:

3 tablespoons extra virgin
   olive oil

1 tablespoon white wine
   vinegar or Champagne
   vinegar

Salt

Black pepper

2 tablespoons finely
   chopped chives

1 Preheat the oven to 375 degrees.

2 Place the beets into a baking dish, drizzle with a little olive oil and shake the pan to coat. Add a good sprinkling of salt and roast for 45–50 minutes, or until tender when pierced with a knife. When cooled to room temperature, peel the beets and slice them horizontally.

3 On a large platter, alternate the beets and oranges in concentric circles.

4 In a small bowl, whisk together the vinaigrette ingredients to form an emulsion. 15 minutes before serving, pour the vinaigrette over the beets and oranges.

Daikon, Watermelon Radish and Beets with Nut Mustard Vinaigrette

Watermelon radish and Chioggia beets are deceptive. From the outside, with their somewhat nondescript skins, they appear rather boring and uninspiring, giving one no indication of the beauty and flavor hiding inside. Once peeled and sliced, the candy cane stripes of the beets and vibrant pink interiors of the radishes are revealed and remind me of extravagant rose petals. I love composing dishes that are visually appealing. I always feel that I am painting a plate when using these vegetables. They make me want to dive right into the dish. Don't skip toasting the pine nuts and pistachios for the salad as the process adds a buttery nuttiness that really transforms the salad.

Serves 8 people

For the salad:

1 small daikon radish—
    peeled, very thinly sliced
    on a mandolin

1 watermelon radish—
    peeled, very thinly sliced
    on a mandolin

1 raw Chioggia beet—
    peeled, very thinly sliced
    on a mandolin

1 raw yellow beet—
    peeled, very thinly sliced
    on a mandolin

1 small head red radicchio—
    leaves separated

1/4 cup pistachios

1/4 cup pine nuts

For the vinaigrette:

1 heaped tablespoon
    nut mustard

1/4 cup extra virgin olive oil

Juice of 1 lemon

1 tablespoon finely
    chopped chives

1 On a large platter, arrange the daikon and beet slices and radicchio leaves in an attractive manner, interspersing the different varieties and colors.

2 Dry roast the pistachios and pine nuts in a small pan over low heat until they release their aroma. Immediately scatter the warm nuts over the vegetables.

3 In a small bowl, whisk together the vinaigrette ingredients to form an emulsion. Pour the vinaigrette over the vegetables and serve.

Salt Roasted Beets with Mackerel and Spiced Onions

Encasing ingredients in salt and then baking them is an age-old cooking technique which helps preserve flavor, moisture and texture. It's often used to cook fish or poultry. You can also prepare carrots, celery root, turnips and parsnips the same way. Here I have used the method to cook beets and the result is magical. When you unearth the beets from the salt, they are tender, sweet and flavorful. The smoked fish adds a salty element to the dish which, when combined with the fragrant and aromatic spices in the *ras el hanout* perfumed onions, creates an exotic dish. This salad is best served when the beets and onions are warm. It is a lovely main course to serve after a chilled soup, such as Zucchini Cappuccino (page 228).

Serves 8 people

8 small yellow beets—unpeeled

1–2 lbs kosher salt

Olive oil

2 red onions—peeled, halved and sliced

1 heaped teaspoon *ras el hanout*

6 oz smoked mackerel (or trout)—skinned, flaked

2 tablespoons cilantro leaves

1 tablespoon chopped dill

2 tablespoons golden raisins

Juice of 1 Meyer lemon

1 Preheat the oven to 400 degrees.

2 Choose a deep baking dish that is just large enough to hold the beets in a single layer. Pour enough salt to create a $1/2$-inch layer. Place the beets onto the bed of salt. Add enough salt to completely encase the beets.

3 Roast in the center of the oven for 45–55 minutes, or until tender when pierced with a knife. Remove the salt from the beets and let them cool slightly. Rinse, peel and slice the beets. Place them in a medium salad bowl.

4 While the beets are roasting, prepare the onions. Heat some olive oil in a medium saucepan. Add the onions and *ras el hanout*. Stir well and cook until the onions are completely softened and golden brown, 12–15 minutes. Add the onions to the salad bowl.

5 Add the mackerel, cilantro, dill and golden raisins to the bowl. Drizzle with a little olive oil and the lemon juice. Gently toss the salad. Divide the salad among eight dinner plates.

Roasted Beets and Butternut Squash with Zesty Parsley Pesto

This is one of my favorite beet dishes. The vibrant pesto is terrific with the rich, roasted butternut squash, the meltingly soft onions and the tender beets. I like to serve this dish with green salad filled with herbs.

Serves 8 people

For the vegetables:

4 red beets—unpeeled

Olive oil

Salt

Black pepper

1 medium butternut squash—
  halved, seeded, peeled,
  cut into 1/3-inch slices

1 large red onion—
  peeled, thinly sliced

1 tablespoon finely
  chopped chives

Zest of 1 lime

For the pesto:

1 cup parsley leaves

1 tablespoon capers

4–5 cornichons

1/4 cup extra virgin olive oil

Zest and juice of 1 small
  Meyer lemon

1 Preheat the oven to 375 degrees.

2 Place the beets in a small baking dish. Drizzle with olive oil, add a good pinch of salt and some pepper, and roast for 50–60 minutes, or until tender when pierced with a knife. When cool enough to handle, peel the beets and slice into 1/3-inch rounds.

3 Pour a little olive oil onto a rimmed sheet pan. Place the butternut squash and onion slices in the pan and turn to evenly coat with oil. Sprinkle with salt and pepper. Roast in the same oven as the beets for 40 minutes.

4 While the vegetables are roasting, make the pesto. Place all the pesto ingredients in a food processor or blender, and purée to a semi-smooth consistency.

5 Arrange the beets, squash, and onions on a large serving platter. Spoon the pesto over the vegetables and sprinkle with the chives and lime zest. Serve warm.

Chioggia Beets with Salmon, Dill, and Crème Fraîche

I like to prepare roasted salmon for dinner parties and special occasions. It multiplies easily, doesn't take long to cook, and makes for an elegant main course. I also like to serve it with a variety of toppings to enhance the dish and vary the flavors. Tossed with dill and crème fraîche, Chioggia beets are unusual, beautiful, slightly earthy, and yet delicate and sweet. When balanced on top of the cooked salmon, they create a dramatic and very pretty presentation. This is the dish I made my lovely mum for Mother's Day.

Serves 8 people

For the beets and salmon:

8–10 Chioggia beets—
   unpeeled

Olive oil

Salt

Black pepper

2½ lbs salmon filet

Juice of 2 lemons

1 tablespoon *herbes de poisson*—or an equal mix of fennel seeds, mustard seeds and coriander seeds

2 lbs baby spinach

2 lemons—quartered

For the vinaigrette:

¼ cup lemon juice
   (Meyer lemon preferred)

1 tablespoon crème fraîche

1 tablespoon finely chopped chives

¼ cup dill—finely chopped

Coarse sea salt

5–6 grinds black pepper

1 Preheat the oven to 375 degrees.

2 Place the beets in a small baking dish. Drizzle with olive oil, add a good pinch of salt and some pepper and roast for 45–50 minutes, or until tender when pierced with a knife. When cooled to room temperature, peel the beets and slice into eighths. Place the beets in a medium bowl.

3 Lower the oven temperature to 350 degrees.

4 Place the salmon onto a rimmed sheet pan or shallow baking dish. Drizzle with a little olive oil, the lemon juice and sprinkle with the *herbes de poisson*. Roast for 15–18 minutes.

5 While the salmon is cooking, prepare the vinaigrette. In a small bowl, whisk together all the vinaigrette ingredients. Pour the vinaigrette over the cooked beets and toss to coat well.

6 Pour a good drizzle of olive oil into a large skillet over medium heat. Add the spinach and cook until just wilted, stirring frequently. Divide the spinach among eight warmed dinner plates.

7 Slice the salmon into eight equal portions and center on the spinach. Top the salmon with the Chioggia beets. Serve with the lemon quarters or squeeze the lemon over each serving. Serve warm.

BRUSSELS SPROUTS, CAULIFLOWER & DARK LEAFY GREENS

Silky Cauliflower Curry Soup

—

Roasted Kale and Brussels Sprouts

—

Warm Cauliflower and
Wilted Spinach Salad

—

Persimmon, Apple and Shaved
Brussels Sprouts Salad

—

Grilled Brussels Sprouts and
Wild Mushroom Salad

—

Multi-Colored Chard and
Purple Kale Salad

—

Roasted Spiced Cauliflower

—

Spring Cauliflower Risotto
with Kale Pesto

—

Cauliflower and Onion Gratin

—

Crispy Kale and Caramelized
Onion Phyllo Tourtes

—

Slow Roasted
Kale-Wrapped Salmon

Silky Cauliflower Curry Soup with Crispy Shaved Brussels Sprouts

Cauliflower is a versatile vegetable that lends itself to all manner of preparations — everything from shaved raw or roasting whole, to being grated for "risotto" or blended for soups. It also absorbs flavors well, but one must be careful not to overpower it with too strong a spice or herb. Curry is a perfect complement to cauliflower, and in this soup it creates a fragrant backdrop for the puréed vegetables. I like to serve puréed soups with a little garnish that provides texture. In this instance, it's the Brussels sprouts which add a little crunch and a lovely earthiness to the gentle, sweet flavor of the cauliflower.

Serves 8 people

For the soup:

2 tablespoons olive oil

1 large yellow onion— peeled and finely chopped

2 leeks—ends trimmed, cleaned, white and light green parts finely chopped

1 tablespoon curry powder

2 heads cauliflower (2 lbs each)—core removed, separated into florets

Salt

Black pepper

8 cups vegetable stock

For the Brussels sprouts:

Olive oil

1 lb Brussels sprouts—finely sliced using a mandolin

Salt

Black pepper

2 tablespoons finely chopped chives

Zest of 1 lemon

1/3 cup crème fraîche

1 Pour the olive oil in a large saucepan over medium heat. Add the onion, leeks and curry powder and cook for 4–5 minutes, stirring frequently until the onions are softened. Add the cauliflower, a good pinch of salt and 10–12 grinds of pepper, and continue cooking for 2 minutes.

2 Add the vegetable stock to the saucepan and simmer until the vegetables are tender, about 20–25 minutes. Remove from the heat and purée the soup using an immersion blender. For a smoother texture, pass it through a fine mesh sieve. Cover and keep the soup warm until ready to serve.

3 Pour a little olive oil into a medium skillet over medium-high heat. Add the Brussels sprouts, a good pinch of salt and 4–5 grinds of pepper. Cook, stirring frequently until the sprouts are golden brown. Add the chives and lemon zest and toss to combine.

4 Serve the soup in warmed soup bowls. Place a dollop of crème fraîche in the center of each bowl and top with a spoonful of the crispy Brussels sprouts.

Roasted Kale and Brussels Sprouts with Dates and Pecans

I like and make a lot of kale salads, but am not a fan of munching through raw kale leaves. Blanching or roasting the kale for a few minutes softens the leaves and makes them easier to digest. This dish is quick and easy to prepare. It is also one of those salads to which you can add lots of ingredients such as feta, grilled chicken or salmon, for a heartier dish.

Serves 8 people

For the vinaigrette:

3 tablespoons olive oil

1 tablespoon Dijon or
	walnut mustard

1 tablespoon red wine
	vinegar

For the vegetables:

1 lb Brussels sprouts—sliced

Olive oil

Salt

Black pepper

1 bunch kale—rinsed, and
	chopped into 1-inch slices

16 pitted dates—
	roughly chopped

1 cup pecans—dry roasted
	for 2 minutes

3 tablespoons finely
	chopped chives

1 Preheat the oven to 350 degrees.

2 In a large salad bowl, whisk together the vinaigrette ingredients to form an emulsion.

3 Place the Brussels sprouts onto a large rimmed sheet pan or into a large shallow baking dish. Drizzle with olive oil and sprinkle with a little salt and 5–6 grinds of pepper. Place in the center of the oven and roast for 10 minutes.

4 Remove the pan from the oven, add the kale and mix with the Brussels sprouts. Return the pan to the oven and continue roasting for 8 minutes.

5 Add the roasted vegetables, dates, pecans and chives to the salad bowl and toss well with the vinaigrette. Serve warm.

Warm Cauliflower and Wilted Spinach Salad

Warm cauliflower and a feta and blue cheese vinaigrette are marvelous together. In fact, the feta and blue cheese vinaigrette is marvelous on just about anything—roasted potatoes, grilled vegetables, haricots verts, asparagus—well, you get the gist. Here it brings everything together in a creamy-tangy-nutty mélange. Yum!

Serves 8 people

For the vinaigrette:

¼ cup olive oil

2 oz feta cheese

1 oz mild blue cheese

Zest and juice of 1 lemon

5–6 grinds black pepper

For the salad:

1 head cauliflower—
   core removed,
   separated into florets

Olive oil

1 lb spinach

Coarse sea salt

Black pepper

¼ cup almonds—
   roughly chopped

¼ cup pistachios—
   roughly chopped

2 tablespoons finely
   chopped parsley

2 tablespoons finely
   chopped dill

1 In a small bowl or mason jar, use an immersion blender to purée the vinaigrette ingredients until completely smooth and homogenous. You can also do this in a conventional blender. Pour the vinaigrette into a medium salad bowl.

2 Steam the cauliflower florets until just tender, about 5–7 minutes. Place in the salad bowl.

3 Pour a little olive oil into a large skillet over medium heat. Add the spinach leaves, a pinch of salt and 4–5 grinds of pepper, and cook for 30 seconds or until just wilted.

4 Add the spinach, nuts, parsley and dill to the salad bowl. Toss well to combine and serve warm.

Persimmon, Apple, and Shaved Brussels Sprouts Salad

This salad is the epitome of autumn on a plate, and it's one of the dishes I like to make when I spy the first Fuyu persimmons of the season at the market. Sweet, crunchy Fuyus and apples counterbalance the raw, earthy flavor of the shaved Brussels sprouts when tossed with a nut mustard vinaigrette.

Serves 8 people

For the vinaigrette:

¼ cup olive oil

1 tablespoon nut mustard

1 tablespoon red wine vinegar

Pinch of coarse sea salt

6–8 grinds black pepper

For the salad:

¼ cup lemon juice

¼ cup olive oil

12 oz Brussels sprouts—uncooked, very thinly sliced on a mandolin

4 Fuyu persimmons—very thinly sliced on a mandolin

4 apples—halved, cored, very thinly sliced

2 tablespoons finely chopped chives

½ cup basil leaves—stacked, tightly rolled and thinly sliced

Zest of 1 lemon

1 In a large salad bowl, vigorously whisk together the vinaigrette ingredients to form an emulsion.

2 In a separate medium bowl, whisk together the lemon juice and olive oil. Add the Brussels sprouts and toss well to coat. Let marinate for 10 minutes.

3 Arrange the persimmon and apple slices with the Brussels sprouts in an attractive pattern in the salad bowl on top of the vinaigrette. Scatter the chives, basil and lemon zest over the vegetables. When ready to serve, very gently toss the salad.

NOTE: A nice variation of this salad includes feta or mild goat cheese crumbled on top.

Grilled Brussels Sprouts and Wild Mushroom Salad

I admit that I was not a Brussels sprouts fan when I was a child in London, not only because the sprouts were boiled to death for our school lunches, but because the lady who lived in the flat beneath us would, on a weekly basis, massacre Brussels sprouts and cabbages together in a putrid, foul, sock-smelling mash, the stench of which permeated the entire house. It took many years not to associate Brussels sprouts with those eye-watering memories. However, the recent craze for grilled Brussels sprouts has gone a long way to curing my resistance. I now cook them throughout the autumn and winter, and love to grate them raw into salads or sauté them until crisp and add them to soups. They are especially delicious paired with mushrooms.

Serves 8 people

For the vegetables:

1¹/₂ lbs Brussels sprouts—halved, blanched for 2 minutes

Olive oil

2 oz butter

1 lb assorted wild mushrooms—ends trimmed, larger mushrooms sliced, small ones left whole

3 tablespoons chopped parsley

2 tablespoons cilantro leaves

For the vinaigrette:

Zest and juice of 1 lemon

3 tablespoons olive oil

Pinch of salt

4–5 grinds black pepper

1 Place the blanched Brussels sprouts in a medium bowl. Drizzle with olive oil and toss to coat.

2 Heat a grill pan over medium-high heat. Grill the Brussels sprouts for 3–4 minutes; turn them once and cook 1–2 minutes more. Transfer the cooked Brussels sprouts to a medium serving platter or shallow bowl.

3 Melt the butter in a large skillet over medium heat. Cook the mushrooms, stirring frequently for 5–6 minutes, or until they are golden brown and begin to render their juice.

4 Add the mushrooms, parsley and cilantro to the serving platter.

5 In a small bowl, whisk together all the vinaigrette ingredients to form an emulsion. Pour the vinaigrette over the vegetables and toss to combine. Serve warm.

Multi-Colored Chard and Purple Kale Salad

I like to add a touch of sweetness to earthy tasting salads, be it with apples or pears or, as in this case, juicy grapes. This is a great dish for a dinner party or large gathering as it can be made well in advance.

Serves 8 people

For the salad:

2 bunches multi-colored chard—ribs removed, sliced into 3/4-inch strips

10–12 green onions— ends trimmed, sliced

Olive oil

Salt

Black pepper

2 bunches purple kale— ribs removed, sliced into 3/4-inch strips

1 cup raw almonds— roughly chopped

1 lb red grapes— halved lengthwise

1 cup cilantro leaves

For the vinaigrette:

1/4 cup olive oil

Juice and zest of 1 large lemon

Pinch of coarse sea salt

5–6 grinds black pepper

1 Preheat the oven to 350 degrees.

2 Place the chard and green onions on a large rimmed sheet pan. Drizzle generously with olive oil, add a sprinkling of salt and 5–6 grinds of pepper. Toss to coat well.

3 Place the kale and almonds on a separate large rimmed sheet pan. Drizzle with a little olive oil, add a sprinkling of salt and 5–6 grinds of pepper. Toss to coat well.

4 Place both sheet pans in the oven and roast the greens for 9 minutes. The kale will have just begun to crisp around the edges.

5 In a large salad bowl whisk together all the vinaigrette ingredients to form an emulsion. Add the cooked vegetables, grapes and cilantro and toss to combine.

NOTE: This salad keeps well and can be made up to an hour in advance.

Roasted Spiced Cauliflower with Yogurt Herb Sauce

There is something quite beautiful about heads of cauliflower with their tight white whorls that resemble puffy cumulus clouds. I am often tempted by them at the market because they are so gorgeous. More than once, I have arrived home and realized that I may have gotten a little carried away in the cauliflower department, and so I set about making soups, salads or simply roasting the florets. This dish came about as a result of one such foray. It is a combination of salty, tangy and sweet flavors, scented with the *ras el hanout* spice mixture.

Serves 8 people

For the yogurt sauce:

8 oz Greek yogurt

2 tablespoons

Zest and juice of 1 lemon

2 tablespoons finely
    chopped chives

Pinch of salt

For the vegetables:

1/3 cup olive oil

1 tablespoon *ras el hanout*

Salt

2 heads cauliflower—cores
    removed, separated into
    small florets

Olive oil

1 large yellow onion—
    peeled, halved and
    thinly sliced

Black pepper

1 cup golden raisins

1/2 cup pine nuts

1/2 cup flat-leaf parsley—
    finely chopped

1   Preheat the oven to 425 degrees.

2   In a small bowl, stir together all the yogurt sauce ingredients. This can be made up to 2 hours in advance and refrigerated until ready to use.

3   In a large bowl, whisk together the olive oil, *ras el hanout* and a large pinch of salt. Add the cauliflower florets and toss to coat well. Place the spiced cauliflower on a rimmed baking sheet and roast until golden brown, about 18 to 20 minutes.

4   While the cauliflower is roasting, prepare the onions. Pour a little olive oil into a medium pan over medium high heat. Add the onions, 5–6 grinds of pepper and cook, stirring frequently until golden brown, approximately 8 minutes. Add the golden raisins and pine nuts and cook 1–2 minutes more.

5   Place the cooked cauliflower, the onion-raisin mixture and parsley in a serving dish, and toss well to combine. Serve with the yogurt sauce.

Spring Cauliflower Risotto with Kale Pesto

Making "risotto" with cauliflower instead of rice lightens the dish but is no less delicious. This version is chock full of vegetables and has a lovely zing to it with the lemony kale pesto.

Serves 8 people

For the pesto:

Olive oil

1 bunch curly kale—rinsed, roughly chopped

Large pinch of coarse sea salt

7–8 grinds black pepper

1/2 cup olive oil

Zest and juice of 2 lemons

1 cup packed Thai basil leaves

For the vegetables:

Olive oil

3–4 baby leeks—trimmed, halved lengthwise, rinsed clean and sliced

16 asparagus— cut into 1/4-inch pieces, tips kept whole

Salt

Black pepper

For the risotto:

Olive oil

1 large onion— finely chopped

Salt

Black pepper

1 large cauliflower— grated or chopped into 1/4-inch pieces

1/4 cup white wine

1 cup vegetable stock

Zest of 1 lemon

1/4 cup toasted pine nuts

4 oz Parmesan or sharp cheddar cheese—grated

2 tablespoons finely chopped chives

1 Drizzle a little olive oil into a large skillet over medium-high heat. Add the chopped kale, salt and pepper and cook for 2–3 minutes, or until the kale is just barely wilted.

2 Place the kale, 1/2 cup olive oil, lemon zest and juice and the basil in the bowl of a food processor fitted with a metal blade, or use an immersion blender to purée the kale into a smooth pesto. Adjust seasoning.

3 Pour a little olive oil into a large skillet over medium heat. Add the leeks and asparagus, and cook for 6–7 minutes or until lightly golden. Season with a little salt and pepper. Keep warm in the pan until the risotto is ready to serve.

4 Pour a little olive oil into a large pan over medium heat. Sauté the onion, stirring occasionally until soft and translucent, about 4–5 minutes. Add the cauliflower, season with salt and pepper and continue to cook for 3–4 minutes.

5 Add the white wine to the cauliflower and cook, stirring constantly, until the liquid has almost evaporated. Add the vegetable stock and bring to a simmer. Cook until the cauliflower is tender, about 6–8 minutes. Remove from the heat and stir in the lemon zest, pine nuts and grated cheese.

6 To serve, spoon the risotto onto each dinner plate. Pour some of the kale pesto into the center of the risotto, top with the spring vegetables, and a sprinkling of chives. Serve immediately with additional grated cheese on the side.

Cauliflower and Onion Gratin

One of the first things my mother taught me to make when I was a little girl was a béchamel sauce. Creamy, luscious and just heavenly, it made everything taste good. My grandmother's version had lashings of crème fraîche in it. It was rich and decadent. I have loved béchamel ever since and often find ways to incorporate it into a dish. My brother and I grew up eating cauliflower gratin. I added onion and shallots to my version, and have found that it's a great way to use up all those small bits of cheese that inevitably get left in the fridge. You can simply grate them all together and add them to the sauce; depending on the cheese, you'll get a slightly different taste each time, but that's part of the charm. And, if you're feeling slightly decadent, add some crème fraîche to the finished béchamel. My grandmother wouldn't have it any other way.

Serves 8 people

Olive oil

1 yellow onion—peeled, halved and thinly sliced

4 shallots—peeled and thinly sliced

1 large cauliflower—core removed, separated into florets and then sliced ¼-inch thick

4 oz prosciutto or thinly sliced ham (optional)— sliced into thin ribbons

2 oz butter

3 heaped tablespoons flour

2 cups milk

2 tablespoons crème fraîche (optional)

6 oz grated Gruyère (or other hard cheese such as cheddar, Manchego or Compté, or all those little bits of cheese left in your fridge)

Large pinch of salt

Black pepper

1 Pour a little olive oil into a large ovenproof skillet over medium heat. Cook the onions and shallots for 2–3 minutes, or until golden.

2 Add the cauliflower slices to the onions and cook for 10 minutes. The cauliflower slices should be barely soft. Stir in the prosciutto and remove from the heat.

3 Preheat the oven to 375 degrees.

4 In a medium saucepan, melt the butter. Add the flour to create a thick paste (roux), and cook about 2–3 minutes, stirring continuously. Add the milk in a slow steady stream, whisking continuously. Stir in the crème fraîche if using. When the sauce has thickened, add the Gruyère cheese, a large pinch of salt and 5–6 grinds of pepper and stir to incorporate.

5 Pour the béchamel sauce over the cauliflower mixture. Bake in the oven for 45 minutes or until the gratin is golden brown.

Crispy Kale and Caramelized Onion Phyllo Tourtes

This recipe may look difficult and complicated, but I promise it isn't, and the result is worth the preparation. I like to serve this pretty tart as part of a brunch buffet or a light lunch.

Serves 8–10 people

1¹/₂ lbs cherry tomatoes

Olive oil

2 teaspoons *herbes de Provence*

3 large onions—peeled, halved and thinly sliced

6 shallots—peeled, halved and thinly sliced

2 teaspoons *herbes de poisson*—or an equal mix of fennel seeds, mustard seeds and coriander seeds

Pinch of salt

Black pepper

2 bunches curly kale—carefully rinsed and chopped into ¹/₂-inch strips

Zest and juice of 1 lemon

10 sheets phyllo dough—thawed

4 oz butter—melted

4 tablespoons pine nuts

2 tablespoons finely chopped chives

2 oz feta cheese—crumbled

2 oz goat cheese—crumbled

1 Preheat the oven to 350 degrees.

2 Place the tomatoes in a medium baking dish. Coat with a little olive oil and sprinkle with the *herbes de Provence*. Roast in the oven for 45 minutes.

3 While the tomatoes are roasting, sauté the onions and shallots in a little olive oil, in a large skillet with the *herbes de poisson*, a good pinch of salt and 4-5 grinds of pepper. Cook until the onions are golden brown. Remove from the heat and let cool to room temperature.

4 Place the chopped kale on a rimmed sheet pan. Drizzle with olive oil and add a good pinch of salt and some pepper. Roast in the oven for 8 minutes. Remove from the oven, toss with the lemon zest and juice, and let cool to room temperature.

5 Increase the oven temperature to 400 degrees.

6 Place the 10 rectangular sheets of phyllo on a dry work surface. Trim to 13-inch square sheets. Reserve the strips for another use.

7 Place one sheet of phyllo on a dry work surface. Keep the remaining sheets of dough covered with a slightly damp cloth to keep them from drying out. Lightly brush the dough with some of the melted butter. Sprinkle with 1 tablespoon of pine nuts.

8 Place a second sheet of phyllo dough on top, pressing down lightly. Lightly brush the dough with some of the melted butter. Sprinkle with 1 tablespoon of chives. Repeat the process with another layer of phyllo and nuts, then a layer of phyllo and chives. Top with a fifth sheet of phyllo and brush with butter.

9 Repeat steps 7 and 8 to make a second 13 x 13-inch stack.

10 Line two 10-inch round tart pans with the phyllo dough. Do NOT trim the edges. Bake for 20 minutes or until a light golden color.

11 Remove the shells from the oven and fill with equal portions of the onion mixture. Spoon the cherry tomatoes evenly over the onions. Sprinkle with the crumbled cheeses.

12 Top the tourtes with the roasted kale and pop them back in the oven for 5 minutes.

Slow Roasted Kale-Wrapped Salmon

The kale in this recipe acts as a seal around the salmon which allows the fish to stay moist and succulent as it cooks. The edges of the kale become crispy, which creates a lovely contrast with the delicate texture of the translucent onions and silken salmon. You can serve this by itself or, if you'd like a little heartier meal, serve the salmon with some rice, couscous or quinoa.

Serves 8 people

Olive oil

4 large red onions—peeled, halved, and thinly sliced

1 bunch green onions— thinly sliced

2 teaspoons *herbes de poisson*—or an equal mix of fennel seeds, mustard seeds and coriander seeds

2 bunches curly kale— tough stalks removed, leaves rinsed and left whole

2 1/2 lbs skinless salmon filet

Coarse sea salt

Black pepper

4 lemons—halved

15–20 toothpicks

1 Preheat the oven to 325 degrees.

2 Pour a little olive oil into a large heavy-bottomed pan over medium heat. Add the red onions, green onions and *herbes de poisson* and cook for 6–7 minutes, stirring frequently, until the onions are soft and translucent.

3 Cover the surface of a large rimmed sheet pan with kale leaves arranged stem end to stem end. Spoon half the onion mixture into the center of the kale bed and place the salmon on top. Spread the remaining onion mixture over the salmon. Sprinkle with salt and pepper. Fold the kale leaves over the salmon and secure with toothpicks.

4 Drizzle the kale-wrapped salmon with a little olive oil. Roast in the center of the oven for 25 minutes.

5 Slice the salmon into eight equal portions and serve on warm plates with a lemon half alongside.

CARROTS

Carrot and Leek Soup
with Zesty Shallots

—

Red Carrot and
Radish Salad
with Toasted Nut
Vinaigrette

—

Shaved Multi-Colored
Carrot Salad

—

Lentils du Puy and
Carrot Salad

—

Trio of Carrot Purées

—

Roasted Acorn Squash
with Carrot "Fries"

—

Roasted Halibut with
Citrus Carrot Purée

—

Clay Pot Chicken
with Carrots, Shallots
and Lemon

Carrot and Leek Soup with Zesty Shallots

My lovely mum made fresh soup almost every day when I was a little girl. We delighted in those big batches of puréed vegetable soups, and mopped up the last remnants in our bowls with big chunks of bread. I have been a big fan of soups ever since. One of my favorites was, and is to this day, carrot soup. This version has leeks in it which add a silky texture and deepens the sweetness of the carrots. I like to make this when the weather is chilly, or perhaps if it's been gray outside for weeks. This soup brings a ray of sunshine and warmth into the kitchen, and warms your tummy.

Serves 8 people

Olive oil

3–4 leeks—halved lengthwise, rinsed clean and finely sliced

1 large yellow onion—peeled, halved and thinly sliced

1 tablespoon fresh thyme leaves

2$1/2$ lbs carrots—peeled and sliced

$1/2$ teaspoon of salt

8–10 grinds fresh black pepper

8 cups vegetable stock

6 shallots—peeled and sliced

2 tablespoons finely chopped chives

Zest and juice of 1 lemon

1 Heat olive oil in a large saucepan over medium heat. Add the leeks, onion and thyme, and cook, stirring frequently until the vegetables are soft and lightly browned, 8–10 minutes.

2 Add the carrots, salt and pepper and cook for 5 minutes. Stir occasionally to ensure that the vegetables do not stick.

3 Add the vegetable stock, reduce heat and simmer for 20 minutes, or until the carrots are soft.

4 Remove from the heat and purée the soup in batches in a food processor or blender or with an immersion blender until smooth. Return the puréed soup to the saucepan and keep warm until ready to serve.

5 Just before serving, prepare the shallots. Warm a little olive oil in a small saucepan or skillet over medium heat. Add the shallots and sauté until golden brown. Add the chives, lemon zest and juice, and cook for 30 seconds more.

6 Top each bowl of soup with a spoonful of the shallot mixture.

Red Carrot and Radish Salad with Toasted Nut Vinaigrette

I spied some exceptionally beautiful carrots one sunny Saturday at the farmers market. These long, thin, red tapered beauties have a hidden golden core which is revealed as you slice them. I couldn't resist. The same farmer also had bunches of breakfast radishes and some particularly fragrant cilantro. Those three ingredients created the foundation for this crunchy salad. I like to serve this with toasted baguette and some salty butter.

Serves 8 people

For the vinaigrette:

1/4 cup pine nuts

1/4 cup pistachios

1 tablespoon olive oil

1 tablespoon walnut or almond oil

1 tablespoon white balsamic vinegar

For the salad:

1 lb red carrots—peeled and finely sliced

1 medium daikon radish—peeled and finely sliced

1 bunch breakfast radishes—peeled and finely sliced

1 cup loosely packed cilantro leaves

3 tablespoons finely chopped chives

Zest of 1 lime

Zest of 1 lemon

1 Place the pine nuts and pistachios in a small skillet over medium heat. Dry roast them until they are just golden brown and releasing their aroma, 1–2 minutes. Whisk in the olive oil, nut oil and vinegar. Pour the vinaigrette into a medium salad bowl. Place serving utensils over the vinaigrette.

2 Place all the salad ingredients on top of the salad utensils. When ready to serve, toss all the ingredients together and divide equally among eight small salad bowls.

Shaved Multi-Colored Carrot Salad

In recent years, rainbow-hued carrots have proliferated at our local markets. From the palest white to sunshine yellow, from dark purple to ruby red, and, of course, the classic orange carrot, they are all hard to resist. Each has its own flavor, and some varieties are noticeably sweeter than others. The carrot shavings transform salads into colorful edible sculptures of crunchy curlicues.

Serves 8 people

3 tablespoons olive oil

Zest and juice of 1 lemon

Pinch of coarse sea salt

4–5 grinds black pepper

1/2 lb (about 4 or 5 medium) multi-colored carrots—peeled

2/3 cup sprouted peanuts

1/2 cup golden raisins

1 cup loosely packed fresh mint leaves

1 In a medium salad bowl, whisk together the olive oil, lemon juice, lemon zest, salt and pepper to form an emulsion. Place salad utensils over the vinaigrette.

2 Using a vegetable peeler, shave the carrots into long, thin ribbons. Place the carrots, peanuts, raisins and mint on top of the salad utensils.

3 When ready to serve, toss the salad well to coat with the vinaigrette.

Lentils du Puy and Carrot Salad

I have to admit I am a little obsessed with these lentils from Auvergne, France. Lentils du Puy are sometimes called the caviar of lentils, and for good reason. They are absolutely worth the premium one pays for them. There are other small French lentils out there, but please trust me when I tell you that these are absolutely the best. They have a slightly nutty, mineral-like quality to them. They can be prepared quickly, and because of their unique characteristics, they retain their shape when cooked, unlike other varieties. Lentils served with a mustardy vinaigrette are classic bistro fare in France and are often served with crispy bacon (lardons) added, or as an accompaniment to duck confit or roast chicken. I love to make variations of this dish by adding assorted vegetables and herbs to the mix. In this version, multi-colored carrots with green onions, parsley and chives are tossed with the lentils and vinaigrette.

Serves 8 people

2 cups lentils du Puy

2 small red onions—
    peeled and quartered

1 bay leaf

4 cups vegetable stock

Coarse sea salt

3 large red carrots—halved
    lengthwise and cut on a
    bias into 1/2-inch slices

3 large orange carrots—
    halved lengthwise and
    cut on a bias into 1/2-inch
    slices

Olive oil

4 green onions—
    thinly sliced

3 tablespoons finely
    chopped parsley

3 tablespoons finely
    chopped chives

Salt

Black pepper

Juice of 1 lemon

1 tablespoon Dijon or
    walnut mustard

1/4 cup olive oil

1 tablespoon red
    wine vinegar

1. Place the lentils, red onions, bay leaf and vegetable stock in a large saucepan. Add a good pinch of salt. Cook covered over medium-low heat for 20–25 minutes, or until the lentils are just *al dente*. Drain and remove the bay leaf. Place the lentils and onions in a medium salad bowl.

2. While the lentils are cooking, steam the carrots until they are just tender, 6–7 minutes. Remove from the steamer and let cool to room temperature.

3. Pour a little olive oil into a large skillet over medium heat. Sauté the green onions, parsley, chives and the cooked carrots. Add a pinch of salt and 4–5 grinds of pepper and cook for 4–5 minutes. Stir in the lemon juice and mix well. Add the carrot mixture to the lentils.

4. In a small bowl, whisk together the mustard, 1/4 cup olive oil and vinegar to form an emulsion. Add the vinaigrette to the lentils and carrots. Mix well. Let sit at least 30 minutes before serving.

Trio of Carrot Purées

Thanksgiving: A day of gratitude with no other agenda than gathering loved ones around a dinner table, enjoying each other's company and delving into an epic feast. I did not grow up with this tradition, but it is one that I readily adopted when I moved from Europe to California, and it has become my favorite holiday.

My first Thanksgivings were for a bunch of French and British ex-pats. We often had twenty or so people around the table, so our feast had a distinctive Anglo-French Mediterranean flavor to it, complete with pâtés, cheese platters, and *Tarte aux Pommes*. Over the last 30 years, the meal has evolved, as have our Thanksgiving traditions. We always begin the meal in the early afternoon, take a break after the main course to go for a long walk, watch the sunset, and return to tuck into all the desserts. As they became older, my children started helping with the preparations and made sure that certain dishes always appeared on the menu. Carrot purée was one of them. Last year, we made three carrot purées using different varieties. Their color was stunning and each had a subtle, yet distinctive flavor. I think we may have started a new tradition.

Serves 8 people

For the red carrot purée:

3 lbs red carrots—
    peeled and cut into
    1/4-inch rounds

2 oz butter

Zest and juice of 1 lemon

Salt and black pepper

For the yellow carrot purée:

3 lbs yellow carrots—
    peeled and cut into
    1/4-inch rounds

2 oz butter

1 tablespoon olive oil

Salt and black pepper

For the orange carrot purée:

3 lbs orange carrots—
    peeled and cut into
    1/4-inch rounds

2 oz butter

3 tablespoons finely
    chopped chives

Salt and black pepper

1 Steam the carrots (keeping the colors separate) for 12–15 minutes, or until quite tender.

2 Separately purée each carrot type with their respective ingredients in a food processor until very smooth. Keep each purée warm in a saucepan or double boiler until ready to serve.

3 Be sure not to omit the lemon juice from the red carrot purée as it helps maintain the carrot's distinctive color.

Roasted Acorn Squash with Carrot "Fries"

I like to eat this as a hearty lunch served with a little green salad. The squash is meltingly tender. You can make a nice variation of the dish by substituting sweet potatoes for the carrots (page 194).

Serves 8 people

4 medium acorn squash—
 halved lengthwise, seeds
 removed

Olive oil

Salt

Black pepper

2 lbs small rainbow carrots—
 peeled and cut into
 1/2-inch wide sticks

2/3 cup pistachios—
 roughly chopped

1 cup Greek yogurt

Zest and juice of 1 lemon

1 tablespoon finely
 chopped chives

1/2 cup parsley leaves

1/2 cup cilantro leaves

1 Preheat the oven to 400 degrees.

2 Place the acorn squash on a rimmed sheet pan cut-side up. Drizzle with a little olive oil, then sprinkle with a little salt and pepper. Bake in the center of the oven until tender, approximately 30–40 minutes.

3 Place the carrots and pistachios in a medium bowl. Drizzle with olive oil, a good pinch of salt and 6–7 grinds of pepper. Toss to coat well. Place the carrots and nuts onto a baking sheet and roast in the oven along with the squash for 20 minutes.

4 While the carrots and squash are cooking, prepare the yogurt mixture. In a small bowl combine the yogurt, lemon zest and juice, a tablespoon of olive oil and the chives.

5 Immediately after removing the cooked carrots from the oven, add the parsley and cilantro leaves to the pan and toss to combine.

6 To serve, spoon some of the yogurt mixture into the hollow of each squash half. Fill with the roasted carrots, standing the "fries" upright in the yogurt mixture. Serve immediately.

Roasted Halibut with Citrus Carrot Purée

I first made this dish for my mother on her birthday. She had requested a quiet dinner party with only a couple of friends. Two days before the party, the guest list ballooned to ten; 24 hours later, we were 16. The menu fluctuated along with the number of guests, but Mum wanted fish for the main course, regardless of the count. Luckily, this dish multiplied easily and the carrot purée could be made ahead of time and warmed up. I often like to cook one ingredient in different ways, served as part of the same dish, so I added some carrot curls for a festive presentation. They provided lovely color, a contrasting texture, and an added depth of flavor. The dish has since become a favorite for parties of any size.

Serves 8 people

For the carrot purée:

1 lb orange carrots—
   peeled and sliced into
   1/4-inch rounds

3 oz butter

Coarse sea salt

Black pepper

1 cup orange juice

Olive oil

6-8 shallots—peeled
   and thinly sliced

1 cup white wine

For the fish:

2 1/2 lbs halibut (or other
   firm white fish)—cut into
   eight equal portions

Salt

Black pepper

Juice of 2 lemons

For the carrot ribbons:

1 lb multi-colored carrots—
   peeled, shaved into long
   thin ribbons

Salt

Black pepper

Zest of 2 limes

1 For the purée, steam the carrots until tender, approximately 7-8 minutes.

2 Place the cooked carrots, 1 oz butter, a good pinch of salt, 5-6 grinds of pepper and the orange juice in a food processor fitted with a metal blade. Process until smooth.

3 Warm a little olive in a medium saucepan. Cook the shallots over medium heat, stirring frequently until soft and lightly golden, approximately 5-6 minutes. Add the white wine and the remaining butter. Cook until the butter has completely melted and the wine has reduced by a third. Stir in the carrot purée. Keep warm in the saucepan until ready to serve.

4 Preheat the oven to 350 degrees.

5 Drizzle a little olive oil into a baking dish large enough to hold all the fish. Place the halibut in the dish and turn to coat. Sprinkle with a good pinch of salt and pepper. Roast for 18-20 minutes. As soon as the fish is cooked through (it will be flaky and completely opaque), pour the lemon juice over the top.

6 For the carrot ribbons, place the carrot shavings on a rimmed sheet pan or baking dish. Drizzle with a little olive oil, sprinkle with a little salt and pepper, and toss to coat. Roast in the same oven as the fish for 10-12 minutes.

7 To serve, warm eight dinner plates. Ladle the carrot purée onto each plate and arrange a piece of halibut in the center. Spoon some of the pan juices over the fish. Top each portion of fish with the carrot ribbons. Sprinkle with the lime zest and serve immediately.

Clay Pot Chicken with Carrots, Shallots and Lemon

Cooking in clay vessels—from Indian biryani pots to the tajines of North Africa to Spanish cazuelas—is a millennium-old technique popular around the world. The pots, which are often soaked in water before using, provide a constant source of moisture for the ingredients as they cook. As a result, clay pots produce fabulously tender, luscious and juicy dishes. Clay pot cooking is also an incredibly healthy cooking method as no oil or butter is necessary. The chicken and vegetables cooked in this dish generate copious amounts of fragrant pan juices, so be sure to serve this in shallow bowls with some lovely bread to soak up all that flavorful broth.

Serves 8 people

6-8 shallots—peeled and
    quartered

3 Meyer lemons—quartered

2 cloves garlic—peeled

2 lbs baby multi-colored
    carrots—peeled

6-8 chicken legs or thighs

5-6 sprigs thyme

Juice of 1 orange

Coarse sea salt

Black pepper

NOTE: Do not preheat the oven. Place the rack in the middle of the oven.

1. Soak a large, unglazed clay pot (top and bottom) in water for 15 minutes; drain.

2. Put the shallots, lemons, garlic and carrots in the bottom of the clay pot. Place the chicken legs on top of the vegetables. Scatter the thyme and pour the orange juice over the chicken. Sprinkle with salt and pepper.

3. Cover with the clay top and place the pot on the center rack of a cold oven.

4. Set the oven to 450 degrees and cook for 1 hour and 15 minutes.

5. Remove the clay pot from the oven and rest it on a wooden surface, cork trivet or folded kitchen towel. A cold surface may cause the clay pot to crack. Lift the lid cautiously, avoiding the steam.

6. Serve the chicken with the lemons and carrots and plenty of the pan juices. Mashed potatoes, rice or simple sautéed greens are delicious paired with this chicken.

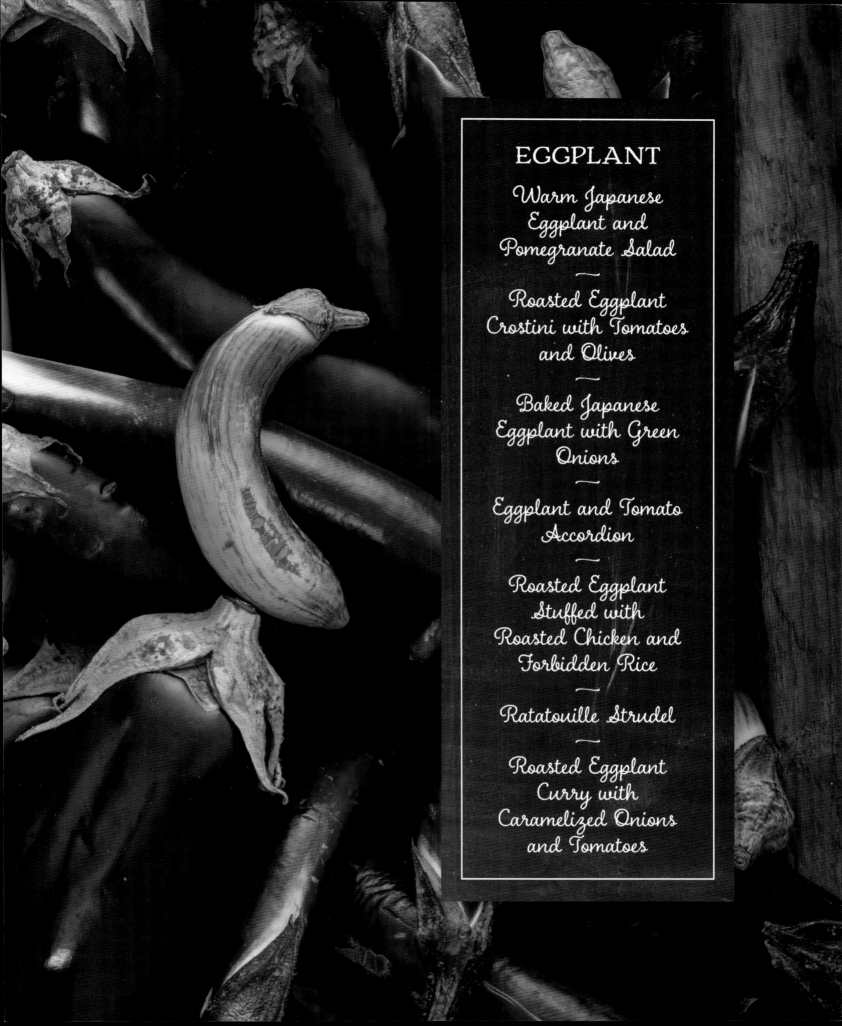

EGGPLANT

Warm Japanese
Eggplant and
Pomegranate Salad

—

Roasted Eggplant
Crostini with Tomatoes
and Olives

—

Baked Japanese
Eggplant with Green
Onions

—

Eggplant and Tomato
Accordion

—

Roasted Eggplant
Stuffed with
Roasted Chicken and
Forbidden Rice

—

Ratatouille Strudel

—

Roasted Eggplant
Curry with
Caramelized Onions
and Tomatoes

Warm Japanese Eggplant and Pomegranate Salad

I first discovered Japanese eggplant at the farmers market in Santa Barbara, drawn to them by their exquisite color and elegant elongated shape. The eggplant I was familiar with did not look anything like these, but it was evident that they came from the same genus. I immediately bought some and went home to experiment. I discovered that they were a creamy, slightly sweet and less bitter version of the more common globe eggplant, and lent themselves well to a plethora of preparations; grilled, sautéed and roasted. The Japanese variety absorbs all types of flavorings and marinades well, and the pomegranate molasses used in this vinaigrette makes the eggplant salad just scrumptious as it soaks into the roasted caramelized slices and coats the pomegranate seeds.

Serves 8 people

Olive oil

8 medium firm Japanese eggplants—sliced into 1/4-inch disks

Large pinch coarse sea salt

Black pepper

3 tablespoons olive oil

1 teaspoon pomegranate molasses

1 teaspoon Jerez vinegar or pear Champagne vinegar

Zest and juice of 1 lemon

1 1/2 cups cilantro leaves

1 cup loosely packed mint leaves

1 1/2 cups loosely packed watercress leaves

1/3 cup finely chopped chives

Seeds from 1 pomegranate

1/2 cup raw peanuts

1 Preheat the oven to 375 degrees.

2 Drizzle a little olive oil over two sheet pans. In a medium bowl, toss the eggplant disks with a little olive oil and spread them on the sheet pans in a single layer. Do not overcrowd the pans or the eggplant will steam instead of evenly caramelize. Sprinkle with a little salt and pepper.

3 Roast, turning the slices once, until golden brown and completely tender, about 25–30 minutes.

4 In a medium salad bowl, whisk together 3 tablespoons olive oil, the pomegranate molasses, vinegar and lemon zest and juice to form an emulsion. Place salad utensils over the vinaigrette.

5 Place the remaining ingredients on top of the utensils. Add the cooked eggplant slices to the salad bowl. Toss to combine well, and serve while the eggplant is still warm.

Roasted Eggplant Crostini with Tomatoes and Olives

Crostini are usually little toasts brushed with olive oil and topped with assorted delicacies. Here, the roasted eggplant slices serve as the toast, and are topped with a creamy yogurt-feta sauce, ripe tomatoes, olives and basil. Try as I might, I cannot eat just one!

Serves 8 people as an appetizer

For the eggplant:

Olive oil

4 medium eggplants—sliced into 1-inch thick disks

1 tablespoon *herbes de Provence*

Salt

Black pepper

For the yogurt sauce:

1/2 cup Greek yogurt

2 tablespoons chopped chives

Juice of 1 small lemon

2 oz feta cheese

2 tablespoons olive oil

4 small yellow cherry tomatoes

For the garnish:

2 medium tomatoes—diced

3 tablespoons black olives—pitted

12 basil leaves—stacked, rolled and sliced

1 Preheat the oven to 375 degrees.

2 Drizzle olive oil onto two rimmed sheet pans. Line the pans with a single layer of the eggplant disks. Do not overcrowd the pans or the eggplants tend to steam instead of roast and caramelize. Drizzle with a little more olive oil. Sprinkle with the *herbes de Provence*, a little salt and 6–7 grinds of pepper.

3 Roast in the center of the oven, turning the eggplants once, for 45 minutes, or until completely tender and golden brown.

4 While the eggplant disks are roasting, prepare the yogurt sauce. Use a blender or immersion blender to purée all of the sauce ingredients until smooth.

5 In a small bowl combine the garnish ingredients and toss well.

6 Place the roasted eggplant disks on a serving platter. Spread some yogurt sauce onto each disk and top with a spoonful of the tomato-olive-basil garnish. Serve warm.

NOTE: These can also be served as part of a main course alongside some couscous, a salad, roast chicken or lamb.

Baked Japanese Eggplant with Green Onions

This is a simple, easy-to-prepare dish that is packed with flavor. It is delicious simply served with yogurt, or you can vary it by adding feta to the mix so the cheese melts in the eggplant as they roast, or by serving it with a spicy tomato sauce on top.

Serves 8 people as a first course or an accompaniment

¼ cup olive oil

1 small bunch green onions—
   finely sliced

1 tablespoon chopped fresh
   lemon thyme

3 tablespoons finely
   chopped chives

4 purple Japanese eggplants

Large pinch coarse sea salt

Black pepper

1 Preheat the oven to 400 degrees.

2 Slit the eggplants lengthwise to create a pocket.

3 In a small bowl, combine the olive oil, green onions, thyme and chives.

4 Place the eggplants in a roasting pan or on a baking sheet. Spoon the mixture into the slit of each eggplant. Drizzle with a little olive oil and sprinkle with salt and 4–5 grinds of pepper.

5 Roast for 35 minutes.

Eggplant and Tomato Accordion

When I hear the undulating, slightly plaintive strains of an accordion, I am instantly transported to France. This has happened to me while sitting in my car listening to the radio, waiting for the light to change. I confess, I may have even closed my eyes for three seconds as *"La Vie en Rose"* played. I dreamt wistfully of eating *soupe au pistou* and *ratatouille* at long, languid meals, bathed in Mediterranean sunlight—only to be awakened by the shrill, incessant horn of the driver behind me. These moments of nostalgia usually have the effect of my wanting to cook something to assuage my intermittent need for all things French. This dish came about as a result of one such craving. I listened to Edith Piaf and Yves Montand as I cooked, and the moment I finished assembling the eggplant and tomatoes, I thought they looked like accordions—hence the name.

Serves 8 people as a first course or an accompaniment

2 large globe eggplants—
quartered lengthwise

5–6 Roma tomatoes—
thinly sliced

5–6 yellow tomatoes—
thinly sliced

Salt

Black pepper

Olive oil

1 tablespoon *herbes de Provence*

1 Preheat the oven to 400 degrees.

2 Place the eggplant quarters onto a baking sheet. Make 10–12 equally spaced parallel cuts across each piece of eggplant. Carefully insert a tomato slice into each cut. Use all red Roma slices in half the eggplants and all yellow tomato slices in the other half.

3 Drizzle the eggplants with olive oil, then sprinkle with the *herbes de Provence*, salt and pepper.

4 Roast for 40 minutes. Serve warm.

NOTE: I particularly like this served with tzatziki, or a tahini-yogurt mixture and a green salad.

Roasted Eggplant Stuffed with Roasted Chicken and Forbidden Rice

Eggplants are the perfect vessels for stuffing. After baking, their shells can be scooped out, mixed with an assortment of ingredients, filled back up, re-heated and served. In this version, the eggplant flesh is combined with roasted chicken and nutty, fragrant forbidden rice. I like to serve this with some wilted spinach or perhaps an arugula salad.

Serves 8 people

Olive oil

3 whole chicken quarters (legs and thighs)

2 tablespoons *herbes de Provence*

Salt

Black pepper

4 12-oz globe eggplants— halved through the stem

1 cup forbidden rice— well rinsed

16 soft dates—chopped

1/3 cup finely chopped chives

1/2 cup cilantro leaves— chopped

1 Preheat the oven to 400 degrees.

2 Pour a little olive oil into a baking dish just large enough to hold the chicken. Turn to coat. Sprinkle with 1 tablespoon of *herbes de Provence*, a good pinch of salt, and 6–7 grinds of pepper. Roast, skin side up, for 1 hour until chicken is tender and falling off the bone. When cool enough to handle, remove the meat from the bones and chop into 1/2-inch pieces. Place in a large bowl.

3 Place the eggplants cut side up on a rimmed baking sheet. Score the cut side of each eggplant half a few times. Drizzle with olive oil and sprinkle the remaining *herbes de Provence*, a good pinch of salt and 5–6 grinds of pepper on top. Roast in the oven, along with the chicken, for 45 minutes. Scoop out the eggplant flesh, leaving 1/2-inch shells. Add the eggplant flesh to the bowl of cooked chicken pieces. Return the shells to the baking sheet.

4 Place the well-rinsed rice in a small saucepan with 11/2 cups of water and a pinch of salt. Bring to a boil. Reduce heat to low. Cover and cook for 20–25 minutes or until the rice is tender and the water has been absorbed.

5 Add the cooked rice to the chicken and eggplant. Stir in the dates, chives and cilantro. Mix well.

6 Fill the eggplant shells with the chicken mixture. Return the filled shells to the oven and bake for 5 minutes. Serve hot.

Ratatouille Strudel

This is a savory version of the classic Austrian dessert. The ratatouille is encased in flaky phyllo dough and baked until golden brown, creating a delicious showstopper.

Serves 8 people

For the ratatouille:

Olive oil

4–5 medium yellow onions— peeled, halved and thinly sliced

1 large or 2 medium eggplants—cut into 1/2-inch cubes

Coarse sea salt

Black pepper

4–6 zucchini—cut into 1/2-inch cubes

8–10 medium Roma tomatoes—diced

3 cloves garlic—minced

1 bay leaf

For the strudel:

10 sheets phyllo dough— thawed

4 oz butter—melted

1/2 cup finely chopped chives

2 bunches watercress— tough stems trimmed

1 Pour a little olive oil into a large heavy-bottomed saucepan or Dutch oven placed over low-medium heat. Add the onions and cook until soft and lightly browned, about 8–10 minutes.

2 While the onions are browning, in a large skillet over medium heat, pour a little olive oil and sauté the eggplant until soft and browned, approximately 8–10 minutes. You may need to do this in batches. Transfer the cooked eggplant to the onions. Season with salt and pepper.

3 In the same large skillet, pour a little more olive oil and add the zucchini. Cook until lightly browned, about 5–7 minutes. Add the cooked zucchini to the eggplant-onion mixture.

4 To the same skillet, add a touch more olive oil and cook the tomatoes and garlic over high heat for 2–3 minutes, until the juice evaporates. Add the tomatoes to the eggplant-zucchini-onion mixture.

5 Continue to cook all the vegetables together with the bay leaf, a large pinch of salt and some pepper for 30–40 minutes, uncovered. Remove the bay leaf just before making the strudel.

6 Unroll the phyllo dough on a flat surface. Place one sheet of the dough on a baking sheet, brush with melted butter and sprinkle with some of the chives. Place a second sheet on top of the first, brush with butter and sprinkle with chives. Repeat with three more sheets.

7 Turn the baking sheet so that the long side is facing you. Spoon half of the ratatouille onto the dough so that it covers one-third of the phyllo lengthwise.

8 Carefully roll the dough to create the strudel, and brush with a little more melted butter. Make a second strudel in the same manner using the rest of the ratatouille and phyllo dough. Place the second one alongside the first and bake in the middle of the oven for 20–25 minutes until golden brown.

9 Remove from the oven and slice each strudel into four pieces. Place each piece onto a warmed dinner plate and serve with some fresh watercress.

Roasted Eggplant Curry with Caramelized Onions and Tomatoes

I am a big fan of vegetable curries and love the fragrant aroma that drifts through the kitchen as the vegetables slowly simmer in the scented broth. Roasting the vegetables before adding them to the broth intensifies their flavor, making the curry rich and savory.

Serves 8 people

1/3 cup olive oil

2 tablespoons curry powder

4 small or 2 large eggplants—
  cut into 1/2-inch cubes

2 large red onions—peeled
  and cut into eighths

1 lb cherry tomatoes

Coarse sea salt

Black pepper

2 tablespoons olive oil

1 yellow onion—peeled,
  halved and thinly sliced

2 cups vegetable stock

2 tablespoons tomato paste

1 cup cilantro leaves

3/4 cup Greek yogurt

1   Preheat the oven to 350 degrees.

2   In a large bowl, whisk together the olive oil and 1 tablespoon of the curry powder. Add the chopped eggplant, red onions and cherry tomatoes and toss to coat well. Place all the vegetables on a large rimmed baking sheet or large roasting pan. Sprinkle with salt and pepper. Do not overcrowd the vegetables or they will steam rather than roast. Use two baking pans if necessary. Roast in the center of the oven for 45 minutes, turning the vegetables once or twice.

3   While the vegetables are roasting, heat 2 tablespoons olive oil in a large saucepan or dutch oven. Add the sliced yellow onions and cook, stirring frequently until they are soft and turning golden brown, about 8–10 minutes. Add the remaining curry powder, vegetable stock and tomato paste. Mix well. Continue to cook 10–15 minutes over low heat.

4   Add the roasted vegetables to the saucepan and stir gently to combine. Simmer the curry for 30 minutes.

5   Spoon the curry into bowls and sprinkle with cilantro leaves and a good dollop of yogurt.

ENDIVES & FENNEL

Chilled Fennel,
Cucumber and Herb
Soup

—

Endives and Smoked
Salmon "Boats"

—

Fennel, Endives
and Cara Cara
Orange Salad

—

Endives, Apple and
Fennel Salad with
Haricots Verts

—

Shaved Fennel Salad
with Asian Pears and
Lime Vinaigrette

—

Braised Endives

—

Endives, Spinach and
Mushroom Gratin

—

Roasted Branzino
with Lemon and
Fennel Fronds

—

Grilled Onion, Endives
and Raw Fennel Salad

Chilled Fennel, Cucumber and Herb Soup

This is the dish I make when it's boiling outside and the thought of cooking anything sends me running from the kitchen. This soup is vibrant, refreshing and perfect for a hot summer's day.

Serves 8 people

For the soup:

1 large fennel bulb—quartered

2 apples—halved

1 large cucumber—peeled

1 head celery

1-inch piece of ginger

2 tablespoons olive oil

Zest and juice of 1 lemon

Salt

Black pepper

For the garnish:

1/2 cucumber—peeled and finely diced

1/2 cup fennel—finely diced

2 tablespoons finely chopped fresh mint leaves

2 tablespoons finely chopped chives

2 tablespoons finely chopped cilantro

1 tablespoon olive oil

Zest and juice of 1 lemon

1 Juice the fennel, apples, cucumber, celery and ginger. Pour the juice into a large pitcher. Stir in the olive oil, lemon zest and juice, a good pinch of salt and 6–7 grinds of pepper. Refrigerate until ready to serve.

2 In a small bowl, mix together all the garnish ingredients.

3 When ready to serve, spoon the garnish into individual soup bowls. If the soup has separated a little, stir it before carefully pouring into the bowls. The garnish will float to the top.

NOTE: I like to serve this with toasted olive bread heaped with ricotta mixed with lemon zest and olive oil.

Endives and Salmon "Boats"

I am surrounded by friends and family who have a penchant for oysters. Despite years of entreaties, I just cannot indulge in bivalves, but I've always appreciated their presentation. I recently saw a documentary on the cuisine of René Redzepi, Danish chef and co-owner of the Michelin two-star restaurant, Noma, and was captivated by the way he plates food using elements of the natural Nordic landscape around him. The next day, I made these salmon "boats" and decided to plate them as I would a platter of oysters with a little Nordic influence. Thank you for the inspiration, René!

Serves 8 people

2 oz crème fraîche

1 heaped tablespoon Greek yogurt

1 tablespoon olive oil

2 tablespoons lemon juice

4 oz smoked salmon— cut into ¼-inch pieces

4 tablespoons finely diced fennel

2 tablespoons chopped dill

2 tablespoons finely chopped chives

2 large Belgian endives— ends trimmed

1 Chill a large serving platter for 30 minutes.

2 In a small bowl, whisk together the crème fraîche, yogurt, olive oil and lemon juice. Add the salmon, fennel, dill and chives, and mix well.

3 Fill the platter with ice.

4 Spoon the mixture into the endive leaves and arrange on the platter.

NOTE: The salmon mixture can be made 2 hours in advance. Keep refrigerated.

Fennel, Endives and Cara Cara Orange Salad

This salad combines the slightly bitter taste of endive leaves with the anise flavored fennel, the sweet, juicy Cara Cara oranges, and the creamy tang of the goat cheese in a sour-salty-sweet mélange that is both zesty and refreshing. If you cannot find the Cara Cara, use either navel or blood oranges.

Serves 8 people

For the salad:

4 Belgian endives—end trimmed, leaves left whole

2 Cara Cara oranges— peeled and segmented

1 large fennel bulb— halved lengthwise, very thinly sliced

1 tablespoon finely chopped chives

¼ cup shelled pistachios

1 teaspoon fennel seeds

2 oz goat cheese— crumbled

For the vinaigrette:

Juice of 1 lemon

2 tablespoons extra virgin lemon olive oil

1 tablespoon almond oil or walnut oil

Pinch of salt

4-5 grinds black pepper

1 Arrange the endive leaves on a large platter. Place orange segments on the endive leaves and scatter the fennel slices on top.

2 Dry roast the pistachios and fennel seed in a small skillet until they begin to release their aroma, approximately 2-3 minutes.

3 Scatter the chives, pistachios, fennel seed and goat cheese on top of the salad.

4 In a small bowl, whisk together all the vinaigrette ingredients to form an emulsion. When ready to serve, drizzle the salad with the vinaigrette.

Endives, Apple and Fennel Salad with Haricots Verts

Last summer, my childhood friend Anya and I spent a few days together at my father's house in the South of France, retracing our steps from summers long ago. We laughed, walked on the beach, read books in the sun, shopped in our favorite market and shared many meals together on the vine-covered terrace. This salad is one I made for us during her visit. Along with the haricots verts, endives and fennel, I used orca beans — an heirloom variety sometimes called calypso beans. They are small, tasty and elegantly dappled in black and white, turning purple and cream colored as they cook. The bean's mild flavor and creamy texture are a nourishing addition to salads, soups and stews.

Serves 8 people

For the salad:

1 cup orca beans—rinsed

1 lb haricots verts

2/3 cup finely diced fennel

1/3 cup shallots—peeled and finely diced

3 tablespoons finely chopped chives

Salt

Black pepper

1 apple (Envy or Fuji)—peeled and diced

1/4 cup almonds—dry roasted, then chopped

1/4 cup pine nuts—dry roasted

5 Belgian endives—ends trimmed

1/2 cup packed basil leaves—stacked, rolled tightly and sliced

For the vinaigrette:

1/4 cup olive oil

1/4 cup yogurt

Zest and juice of 1 lemon

2 tablespoons finely chopped flat-leaf parsley

1 Place the orca beans in a large saucepan with 4 cups of cold water. Cover and bring to a boil. Reduce heat to medium-low and cook until tender, about 50-60 minutes. Check to be sure the beans are covered with water during cooking. Add more if necessary. Drain and rinse under cold water.

2 Steam the haricots verts until just tender, approximately 6-7 minutes. Remove from the steamer and rinse under cold water.

3 In a medium bowl, combine the fennel, shallots, chives, a good pinch of salt and 6-7 grinds of pepper. Let rest for 5 minutes. Add the cooked orca beans, diced apple, almonds and pine nuts. Mix well.

4 In a small bowl, whisk together all the vinaigrette ingredients. Pour the vinaigrette over the beans and apples. Toss well to combine.

5 To plate the salad, arrange the endive leaves and haricots verts around the perimeter of a large shallow platter, alternating between 5-6 endive leaves and several haricots verts. Spoon the orca bean mixture into the center of the platter, encircling it with the basil chiffonade.

Shaved Fennel Salad with Asian Pears and Lime Vinaigrette

Every time I make this dish, I am reminded of calla lilies. Like the flowers, this salad is elegant and beautiful. It is a crisp and refreshing way to start any meal. The lime vinaigrette adds a floral note and a little unexpected zing to the dish.

Serves 8 people

1 large fennel bulb—peeled, quartered lengthwise, very thinly sliced on a mandolin

2 Asian pears—peeled, halved, cored, very thinly sliced on a mandolin

3 tablespoons olive oil

Zest and juice of 1 lime

Salt

Black pepper

3-4 sprigs dill— stems removed

1 On a large plate or shallow dish, arrange the fennel and pear slices, intertwining them.

2 In a small bowl, whisk together the olive oil, lime zest and juice, a pinch of salt and 3-4 grinds of pepper. Drizzle over the salad.

3 Sprinkle the salad with dill leaves and serve.

Braised Endives

I never really liked endives as a child, finding them too bitter. Now I can't get enough of them whether cooked or raw. This simple preparation is one of my favorites, and the endives can be served with everything from a spinach salad to roasted duck. As the endives braise, they become meltingly soft and buttery, and are oh so delicious. I can eat an entire dinner of just these!

Serves 8 people

8 Belgian endives—
  halved lengthwise

Olive oil

1 tablespoon butter

Salt

Black pepper

1 tablespoon finely
  chopped chives

1 In a skillet large enough to hold all the endive halves in one layer, heat a little olive oil and the butter until sizzling. Add the endive halves and brown on both sides, approximately 3–4 minutes per side. Add a good pinch of salt and 8–9 grinds of pepper.

2 To braise the endives, add 1 cup of water to the skillet. Cover, reduce heat to low and cook for 15–20 minutes, turning occasionally. Be sure there's enough water to cover the bottom of the skillet.

3 Sprinkle with chives just before serving.

Endives, Spinach and Mushroom Gratin

This gratin is one of the more decadent preparations for this elegant vegetable. The endives are covered with layers of spinach and mushrooms and a mouth-watering mornay sauce.

Serves 8 people

Olive oil

4 firm Belgian endives—
halved lengthwise

Salt

Black pepper

1 lb spinach

2 tablespoons chopped
chives

4 oz butter

1½ lbs brown mushrooms—
sliced

3 heaped tablespoons flour

2 cups milk

4 oz Gruyère cheese—
grated

1   Preheat the oven to 375 degrees.

2   Pour a little olive oil into a large, deep ovenproof skillet over medium heat. Add the endive halves in one layer and brown on both sides, approximately 3–4 minutes per side. Add a good pinch of salt, 8–9 grinds of pepper.

3   Add 1 cup of water to the skillet. Cover, reduce heat to low and cook for 15–20 minutes, turning occasionally. Be sure there's enough water to cover the bottom of the skillet.

4   Pour a little olive oil into a large pan over high heat. Add the spinach and cook until just wilted. Spoon the spinach over the endives and sprinkle with chives.

5   Using the same pan, melt 1 ounce (2 tablespoons) of butter. Sauté the mushroom slices until golden brown. Sprinkle with a little salt. Spoon the mushrooms over the spinach.

6   In a medium saucepan, melt the remaining butter. Add the flour to create a thick paste (roux), and cook about 2–3 minutes, stirring continuously. Add the milk in a slow steady stream, whisking continuously. When the sauce has thickened, add half the Gruyère cheese, a large pinch of salt and 5–6 grinds of pepper, and stir to incorporate.

7   Pour the cheese sauce over the mushrooms. Sprinkle with the remaining cheese

8   Bake in the center of the oven for 10–15 minutes, or until golden brown. Serve hot.

Roasted Branzino with Lemon and Fennel Fronds

This tasty, quick preparation for the Branzino infuses the fish with the scent of the fennel. This is one of my favorite ways to prepare whole fish.

Serves 8 people

Olive oil

Fronds from 2 large fennel bulbs

4 Branzino (12–16 oz each)—gutted and cleaned

4 lemons—thinly sliced

Salt

Black pepper

1 Preheat the oven to 375 degrees.

2 Place the fennel fronds on a lightly oiled, rimmed baking sheet. Arrange the branzini side by side, head to tail, on the fennel fronds. Top the fish with the lemon slices, slightly overlapping. Drizzle with olive oil, sprinkle with salt and pepper.

3 Roast in the center of the oven for 25–30 minutes, or until the flesh is completely opaque and comes away from the bone easily.

4 To plate, debone the fish and place one filet on each dinner plate. Serve with the salad alongside.

Grilled Onion, Endives and Raw Fennel Salad

I like the juiciness of grilled vegetables mixed with the crunch of raw ones. I often serve this salad with grilled or whole roasted fish; it also pairs well with any roast or as a first course.

Serves 8 people

1/4 cup olive oil

Juice of 1 lemon

1 tablespoon Dijon mustard

Olive oil

3 large red onions—peeled, thinly sliced into disks

1 tablespoon *herbes de poisson*—or an equal mix of fennel seeds, mustard seeds and coriander seeds

4 Belgian endives—halved lengthwise

2 fennel bulbs—very thinly sliced

1/3 cup pistachios—chopped

1/3 cup golden raisins

1/4 cup finely chopped chives

1 In a large salad bowl, vigorously whisk together 1/4 cup of olive oil, the lemon juice and mustard to form an emulsion.

2 Pour a little olive oil into a medium mixing bowl. Add the onions and *herbes de poisson* and toss to coat.

3 Heat a grill pan over high heat. Grill the onion slices until lightly browned on both sides. Add to the salad bowl.

4 Pour a little more olive oil into the same mixing bowl. Add the endive halves and toss to coat. Grill the endives for 2–3 minutes on each side. Add to the salad bowl.

5 Add the fennel, nuts, raisins and chives to the salad bowl. When ready to serve, toss to coat well.

LEEKS, ONIONS & SHALLOTS

Onion Marmalade Crostini

~

Steamed Leeks with a Chive
and Shallot Vinaigrette

~

Ragout of Spring Leeks,
Shitake and Peas

~

Sauté of Leeks and Snap
Peas with Burrata

~

Smoked Salmon, Leek
and Lemon Tartelettes

~

Braised Leek, Shallot
and Onion Soup

~

Spring Vegetable Tagine
with Za'atar

~

Whole Roasted Red Onions
with Feta and Crispy
Brussels Sprouts

~

Roasted Onion, Olive
and Pesto Tart

~

Mustardy Chicken
with Buttery Leeks

Onion Marmalade Crostini with Arugula and Goat Cheese

These crostini are equally scrumptious made with goat cheese or with a blue cheese such as gorgonzola or Roquefort. Either way, they are easy to prepare and a lovely sweet-savory way to begin a meal.

Serves 8 people as an appetizer

Olive oil

2 large onions—peeled and finely diced

1 teaspoon *herbes de Provence*

Large pinch coarse sea salt

8-10 grinds black pepper

¼ cup white wine vinegar or Champagne vinegar

1 tablespoon honey

8 pieces of toasted baguette

2 oz goat cheese—crumbled

1 cup baby arugula leaves

1 Pour a little olive oil into a medium saucepan over medium heat. Add the onions, *herbes de Provence*, salt and pepper and cook for 3-4 minutes, stirring frequently until the onions start to soften and color. Reduce the heat to low and continue cooking until the onions are golden brown, about 20 minutes.

2 Add the vinegar and honey and cook for 10-15 minutes, stirring occasionally so that the onions do not catch. The marmalade will be thick and sticky.

3 Spoon a little of the marmalade onto the toasted baguette slices. Top with the goat cheese and a few arugula leaves.

Steamed Leeks with a Chive and Shallot Vinaigrette

I grew up eating the classic French dish, *poireaux vinaigrette*, at my grandmother's house. In this version, I've cut the leeks into small chunks to create an easy-to-munch appetizer. This is one of my favorites.

Serves 8 people as an appetizer

For the leeks:

4 long leeks—trimmed, rinsed, white and light green parts sliced into 1-inch pieces. Reserve the trimmings for stock

For the vinaigrette:

¼ cup olive oil

1 tablespoon white wine vinegar

1 shallot — peeled and finely diced

1 tablespoon finely chopped chives

Coarse sea salt

Black pepper

1 Using a vegetable steamer, cook the leek pieces for 7-8 minutes. They should be soft, yet still hold their shape. Place the cooked leeks on a serving plate.

2 Whisk the vinaigrette ingredients together in a small bowl. Pour the vinaigrette over the leeks and let rest at least 10 minutes before serving. Serve at room temperature.

Ragout of Spring Leeks, Shitake and Snap Peas

This stew is filled with rich flavors from the sautéed shitake mushrooms and the salty, smoky chorizo. If you want to make a strictly vegetarian version, omit the sausage and add more wild mushrooms.

Serves 8 people

Olive oil

1 tablespoon butter

4–5 long thin leeks—
   trimmed, cleaned and
   sliced ¼-inch thick

1 lb snap peas—cut on a bias

¼ cup white wine

2 cups vegetable broth

1 bunch pea shoots—
   roughly chopped

1 lb shitake mushrooms—
   stems trimmed and caps
   cut in half

⅓ lb Spanish chorizo—
   cut into ¼-inch slices

1 Heat a little olive oil and the butter in a large saucepan over medium heat. Add the leeks and cook for 7–8 minutes, stirring occasionally and turning once or twice. Add the snap peas and cook for 2 minutes. The leeks should be soft and lightly golden, and the snap peas still crunchy.

2 Pour in the wine and cook until it has evaporated. Add the broth and pea sprouts and cook for 3–4 minutes. Remove from the heat.

3 Melt 2 tablespoons of butter in a large skillet over medium-high heat. Add the mushrooms and sauté until golden brown. 4–5 minutes.

4 Gently combine the cooked mushrooms and the chorizo slices with the leek and snap pea mixture.

5 Serve immediately. Be sure each person receives some of the broth with the vegetables.

Sauté of Leeks and Snap Peas with Burrata and Lemon Olive Oil

This is one of my favorite dishes in this book. I first made it for a cooking class I taught a few years ago after having come across some truly beautiful, long, long leeks at the market. I steamed some to serve with a vinaigrette, and then set about experimenting with the rest. This dish is the result of those experiments. It became an instant favorite. My good friend Nancy called to tell me she made this and added it to fresh pasta, which inspired me to do the same. It's utterly delectable, especially with fettucine or pappardelle.

Serves 8 people

Olive oil

4 leeks—trimmed, rinsed, white and light green parts cut into 1/2-inch pieces

1 lb snap peas—cut on a bias into 1/2-inch pieces

Zest and juice of 1 lemon

1/2 cup finely chopped chives

1/4 cup lemon olive oil

Salt

Black pepper

1 fresh burrata

1 Pour a little olive oil into a large skillet over medium-high heat. Sauté the leeks for 3–4 minutes, stirring frequently. Add the snap peas and cook for 3–4 minutes. The snap peas should be *al dente*.

2 In a large salad bowl, whisk together the lemon juice, zest and 1/4 cup olive oil. Add a pinch of salt and 4–5 turns of pepper and whisk again. Place salad utensils over the vinaigrette. Place the vegetables on top of the utensils and sprinkle with the chives.

3 Tear the burrata into chunks and add it to the salad. Toss to combine and serve immediately.

Smoked Salmon, Leek and Lemon Tartelettes

These elegant little tarts are rich, savory and buttery with just a smidge of tanginess. I like to serve them with a peppery salad made with arugula and frisée.

Serves 8 people

For the short crust pastry:

9 oz (2 cups) unbleached all-purpose flour

5 1/2 oz butter—chilled, cut into small pieces

1 large egg

Zest of 1 lemon

Pinch of salt

4–5 grinds black pepper

For the smoked salmon mixture:

2 tablespoons (1 oz) butter

1 tablespoon olive oil

4 leeks—trimmed, halved lengthwise, rinsed clean, white and light green parts thinly sliced

3 tablespoons finely chopped chives

1/2 cup crème fraîche

1/4 cup yogurt

1/2 lb smoked salmon—cut into 1/2-inch strips

Zest and juice of 1 lemon

1 Preheat the oven to 400 degrees. Butter eight 4-inch tartelette pans.

2 Place all the ingredients for the short crust pastry in the bowl of a food processor fitted with the metal blade. Pulse until the mixture resembles coarse breadcrumbs. Use longer pulses until the dough forms a ball. Wrap the dough in plastic wrap and refrigerate for 20 minutes.

3 Divide the dough into eight portions. On a lightly floured board, roll out the dough into disks, 1/4-inch thick. Line the tartelette pans with the dough. Trim the edges with a sharp knife and prick the dough with a fork. Line the dough with a piece of parchment paper and fill with pie weights or dried beans. Bake for 12–14 minutes until they are just golden. Carefully remove the parchment paper and pie weights.

4 In a medium skillet, over medium high heat, melt the butter with the olive oil. When it begins to foam, add the leeks and cook for 7–8 minutes. The leeks should be soft but still retain some of their vibrant color.

5 In a medium bowl, mix the chives, crème fraîche, yogurt and smoked salmon. Add the cooked leeks, the zest and lemon juice, and stir to combine well.

6 Fill each partially baked tartelette shell with the smoked salmon-leek mixture. Return to the oven and finish baking for 10–15 minutes, or until the crust is golden brown. Serve warm.

Braised Leek, Shallot and Onion Soup

I have never been a fan of classic French onion soup, at least not the version with endlessly long strands of rubbery melted cheese that are impossible to disconnect from the bowl. I do love the flavors of the soup however, so this is my version, sans cheese!

Serves 8 people

Olive oil

4–5 long thin leeks—
ends trimmed, halved
lengthwise and cleaned,
white and light green
parts thinly sliced

6–8 small shallots—
peeled and sliced

7 cups vegetable stock

2 lbs small (red and yellow)
pickling onions—
blanched, peeled
and quartered

4–5 sprigs thyme

1 teaspoon salt

5–6 grinds black pepper

4–6 green onions—ends
trimmed and thinly sliced

2 tablespoons thinly
sliced chives

1 Pour a little olive oil into a large saucepan over medium heat. Add the leeks and shallots and cook, stirring frequently for 3–4 minutes. Add 1 cup of vegetable stock and cook covered until the vegetables are completely soft, about 6–8 minutes.

2 Add the onions, thyme, salt, pepper and the remaining stock. Simmer for 15 minutes.

3 Gently stir in the chopped green onions and chives and let simmer for 2 minutes. Serve in warmed soup bowls.

Spring Vegetable Tagine with Za'atar

Please don't be put off by the lengthy ingredient list. This recipe is actually quite simple—it's mostly just chopping—and the result is an aromatic, succulent stew. I like to accompany this dish with a date and herb filled couscous. Oh, and don't skimp on the yogurt; it adds zing to the tagine.

Serves 8 people

For the za'atar:

1/4 cup olive oil

1 small bunch fresh oregano—finely chopped

1 small bunch fresh thyme—finely chopped

1 teaspoon sumac

1 teaspoon sesame seeds

For the tagine:

1 red onion—peeled, halved and thinly sliced

3-4 leeks—trimmed, rinsed, white and light green parts sliced 1-inch thick

4-5 green onions—trimmed and cut into 1/2-inch pieces

4 shallots—peeled and quartered

Salt and black pepper

1 lb asparagus—cut on a bias into 1-inch pieces

1/2 lb baby spinach leaves

1 lb snap peas—cut into 1/2-inch pieces

1/3 cup golden raisins

3 cups vegetable broth

For the lemon yogurt:

2 cups Greek yogurt

1 or 2 preserved lemons—chopped

1 tablespoon olive oil

7-8 grinds black pepper

1 pinch paprika

1 pinch curry powder

1 Preheat the oven to 350 degrees.

2 Combine 1/4 cup olive oil, the oregano, thyme, sumac and sesame seeds in a small bowl to create the fresh *za'atar*.

3 Place the red onion, leeks, green onions and shallots on a rimmed sheet pan. Pour the *za'atar* over the vegetables and toss to coat well. Sprinkle with salt and pepper. Roast on the center rack for 30 minutes.

4 Place the roasted vegetables in an extra-large, stovetop tagine or dutch oven, over medium heat. Stir in the asparagus, spinach, snap peas and golden raisins. Add the vegetable stock. Cover and cook over medium heat for 10 minutes.

5 In a small bowl, stir together all of the lemon yogurt ingredients. Let rest at least 30 minutes for the flavors to meld. Serve alongside the tagine.

Whole Roasted Red Onions with Feta and Crispy Brussels Sprouts

John Evelyn, the English writer, gardener and 17th century diarist, wrote, amongst other things, the first known, definitive work on salads, Acetaria: A Discourse on Sallets. In it he details the attributes of some 70-plus herbs, greens and vegetables and the methods for their respective preparations. He writes enthusiastically about all forms of alliums, particularly whole, baked onions, "An honest laborious country man, with good bread, salt and a little parsley, will make a contented meal with a roasted onion." I agree with him whole-heartedly. Roasting onions in their skins transforms them into tender, soft, sweet vegetables to which one can add a plethora of ingredients. You can serve these onions as part of a larger vegetarian meal, as an accompaniment to any roast, or as Mr. Evelyn would suggest, with simply a plain green salad.

Serves 8 people

8 large red cippolini onions—
  rinsed clean, left unpeeled

Olive oil

8-10 Brussels sprouts—
  trimmed and thinly sliced

Salt

Black pepper

2 oz feta cheese—crumbled

1 Preheat the oven to 375 degrees.

2 Place the onions in a shallow baking dish and drizzle with a little olive oil. Roast 45–50 minutes or until completely soft when pierced with a knife. Let cool, trim ends and peel the outer layer. Slice each onion vertically down the middle, stopping 1/2 inch from the bottom.

3 Heat a little olive oil in a small skillet over medium heat and add the Brussels sprouts, a pinch of salt and some pepper. Cook, stirring frequently, until browned and lightly crispy, about 5–6 minutes. Remove from the heat, let cool for 1–2 minutes and then stir in the feta.

4 Spoon the Brussels sprouts-feta mix into each onion and serve warm.

Roasted Onion, Olive and Pesto Tart

As a young teenager, I was tennis mad, obsessed even. My father decided one summer to channel that enthusiasm into a tennis camp. The entire family went, each of us whacking tennis balls for six or seven hours a day. The camp, being in France, wasn't solely focused on athletics. If one exercised that much, they reasoned, one should also be well fed. Lunch breaks were two hours—time to eat, digest, and have a little siesta, before returning to the court. It was during one of these long breaks that I discovered the magic of making puff pastry. I was invited to watch the chef make this extraordinary dough. He served the baked delicacy sliced in half and spread with a Roquefort-butter concoction that melted into the buttery layers. It was divine. I have been as infatuated with this dough as with tennis ever since.

Serves 8 to 10 people

For the onions:

Olive oil

2 red onions—peeled
    and thinly sliced

2 yellow onions—peeled
    and thinly sliced

Coarse sea salt

Black pepper

For the pesto:

Zest and juice of 1 large
    lemon

1/2 cup olive oil

2 cups basil leaves

For the tart:

1 sheet frozen puff pastry—
    thawed

1 bunch green onions—
    chopped

1/2 cup assorted olives—
    pitted

2 oz feta cheese—crumbled

1 Preheat the oven to 400 degrees.

2 Pour a little olive oil onto a rimmed sheet pan or into a shallow baking dish. Arrange the onions in a single layer. Sprinkle with a little salt and pepper. Drizzle with just a little olive oil. Roast the onions until golden brown, about 15-20 minutes. Remove and let cool.

3 While the onions are roasting, prepare the pesto. Using a blender or food processor, chop the basil leaves, then add the lemon juice and olive oil to create a thick paste. Add a pinch of salt and some pepper, scrape down the sides and blend again.

4 Unfold the puff pastry onto a lightly floured piece of parchment paper and gently roll it out into a 9 x 12-inch rectangle. Place the parchment with the pastry onto a baking sheet. Bake until lightly golden brown, approximately 15 minutes. Remove from the oven and let cool slightly.

5 Carefully spread a thin layer of pesto over the partially cooked pastry, leaving a 1/2-inch border. Cover the pesto with the roasted onions and scatter with the green onions and olives.

6 Return the tart to the oven and continue baking for 10-15 minutes. The tart should be golden brown. Remove the tart from the oven and immediately top with the crumbled feta. I like to serve this with a green salad.

NOTE: This recipe makes more pesto than you will need for the tart. Reserve the remainder for pasta or as a lovely addition to risotto.

Mustardy Chicken with Buttery Leeks

The essence of this chicken dish stems from a sauce I learnt to make with my grandmother. Every time I visited her, she would make *lapin a la moutarde* or rabbit with mustard sauce. That rich sauce was worthy of a journey across the country. At the end of the meal, the family would jockey for position to clear the dishes, in particular, the platter that had held this magnificent creation, as there would always be remnants of that delectable, mustardy, crème fraîche concoction in the bottom, begging for a piece of baguette to mop it up. Woe betide you if you got caught doing that. But I think that was half the fun—an illicit dredging of the platter with a hastily torn piece of bread. Ah, bliss. Be sure to serve this with some hearty bread so that you, too, can soak up all that deliciousness.

Serves 8 people

For the chicken:

1 tablespoon Dijon mustard

Salt

Black pepper

4 chicken drumsticks

6–8 chicken thighs

Olive oil

1 cup vegetable stock

For the leeks:

6 leeks—trimmed, rinsed, white and light green parts cut into ½-inch pieces

5–6 green onions— finely sliced

1 tablespoon Dijon mustard

3 tablespoons crème fraîche

1 cup vegetable stock

1 Mix the mustard with a large pinch of salt and 4–5 grinds of pepper in a medium bowl. Add the chicken pieces and toss to coat.

2 Heat a little olive oil in a large, deep pan. Brown the chicken pieces on all sides, approximately 5–7 minutes. Add the vegetable stock, cover, lower the heat and simmer for 20 minutes, turning the pieces once or twice.

3 In a separate large pan, heat a little olive oil and cook the leeks and green onions, stirring frequently until just soft, about 5 minutes.

4 In a small bowl, blend the Dijon mustard, crème fraîche and vegetable stock. Stir into the leeks and cook for 2 minutes.

5 Add the leek mixture to the chicken and let simmer for 10–15 minutes. Serve hot.

MUSHROOMS

Wild Mushroom
Soup with Sautéed
Enoki and Crispy Kale

—

Wild Mushroom and
Taleggio Crostini

—

Warm Roasted
Mushroom Salad
with Arugula and
Watercress

—

Forbidden Rice "Field"
with Sauté of Warm
Mushrooms

—

Grilled Mushroom,
Snow Pea and Bok
Choy Salad

—

Tagliatelle and
Chanterelles

—

Mushroom and
Asparagus Quiche

Wild Mushroom Soup with Sautéed Enoki and Crispy Kale

This soup is a celebration of autumnal flavors and savory textural contrasts with a rich and creamy mushroom purée, sautéed enoki and crispy kale.

Serves 8 people

Olive oil

2 leeks—halved lengthwise, rinsed, cleaned and finely sliced

2 shallots—peeled and thinly sliced

3 oz butter

1 lb crimini mushrooms—sliced

1 lb white button mushrooms—sliced

4 cups vegetable stock

1 teaspoon salt

Black pepper

1 lb enoki mushrooms—separated

1 bunch dinosaur kale—rinsed, cut into 1/2-inch wide strips

2 tablespoons finely chopped chives

1 Pour a little olive oil into a large saucepan over medium heat. Sauté the leeks and shallots, stirring frequently until golden brown, approximately 7–8 minutes.

2 Add half the butter to the leeks. When the butter has melted completely, add the mushrooms and cook for 15 minutes, stirring often.

3 Add the vegetable stock, salt and 6–7 grinds of pepper. Simmer for 10 minutes. Use an immersion blender to purée the soup. Cover and keep warm.

4 Preheat the oven to 350 degrees.

5 Melt the remaining butter in a small skillet over medium heat. Add the enoki mushrooms and cook, stirring frequently for 7–8 minutes, until they are completely golden.

6 Place the kale on a rimmed sheet pan. Drizzle with olive oil. Add a good pinch of salt and some pepper and toss to coat. Roast for 8–10 minutes until just crispy.

7 To serve, ladle the soup into eight warmed bowls. Top with the kale and enoki mushrooms. Sprinkle with chives.

Wild Mushroom and Taleggio Crostini

Many moons ago, I spent a summer baking cakes and tarts for some restaurants in the South of France. The fruits of my labor funded my first visit to the magical city of Venice. I spent days wandering through its maze-like streets, buying lunch from the floating vegetable markets on the canals—usually some grapes, a little cheese and perhaps some grissini and prosciutto—discovering ancient churches and silent medieval squares. I was enchanted by every corner and walked for hours. If I was feeling peckish, I would pop into a bacari, a small wine bar, for sustenance in the form of cicchetti, the small snacks coveted by the Venetians. There would be a wide assortment of small toasts with fish, cheese or olives on top, and small plates of marinated vegetables, grilled peppers and mushroom crostini—my favorite. Most of these places were standing-room only, and packed with locals who would pass little plates filled with regional delicacies to one another. The recipe for these crostini was inspired by that visit.

Serves 8 people as an appetizer

Butter

2 lbs assorted wild mushrooms—cleaned carefully and sliced

Salt

Black pepper

1 tablespoon finely chopped chives

1 tablespoon finely chopped parsley

8 slices ciabatta bread— lightly toasted

Lemon olive oil

2 oz goat cheese

6 oz Taleggio or fontina cheese—cut into small pieces

1. Melt 1 tablespoon of butter in a large skillet over medium heat. In batches, sauté the mushrooms until golden brown, about 5–8 minutes. Once all the mushrooms are cooked, return them to the pan. Add a large pinch of salt, 8–9 grinds of pepper, the chives and parsley. Mix well, then remove from the heat.

2. Place the toasted ciabatta on a rimmed baking sheet. Drizzle each slice with a little lemon olive oil. Spread with the goat cheese and heap the mushrooms on top. Dot each crostini with pieces of Taleggio. Place under the broiler for 3–4 minutes or until the cheese has melted. Serve hot.

Warm Roasted Mushroom Salad with Arugula and Watercress

On a recent trip to London, I visited Southwark's Borough Market, a market which has existed in one form or another for more than a thousand years. The many artisans, bakers and farmers stands were arrayed in a partially covered atrium. It was here that I spied the most extraordinary and diverse selection of wild mushrooms, including Pied Bleu with their blue-purple stems, golden chanterelles, buckets of morels and the pale-stemmed king trumpets. Alas, as I was travelling through London that day and had no opportunity to cook, I could only admire and photograph the stunning fungi. Those photos inspired this salad. You can use any type of mushroom, but do try and find a nice variety as it will add richness and depth to the dish.

Serves 8 people

For the salad:

2¹/₂ lbs assorted mushrooms, including cremini, trumpet, enoki, shitaki—sliced

Olive oil

Salt

Black pepper

4 oz watercress— ends trimmed

4 oz baby arugula

For the vinaigrette:

1 tablespoon walnut mustard

¹/₄ cup extra virgin olive oil

1 tablespoon Champagne or white wine vinegar

1 Preheat the oven to 350 degrees.

2 Place the mushrooms on a rimmed baking sheet or shallow baking dish large enough to hold them in one layer. Drizzle with olive oil and sprinkle with salt and pepper. Roast for 30 minutes.

3 While the mushrooms are roasting, assemble the rest of the salad. In a large salad bowl whisk together the vinaigrette ingredients to form a thick emulsion. Place salad utensils over the vinaigrette.

4 Place the watercress and arugula on top of the utensils.

5 As soon as the mushrooms are cooked, add them to the salad bowl. Toss to combine well. Serve while the mushrooms are still warm.

Forbidden Rice "Field" with Sauté of Warm Mushrooms

I awoke one morning this past winter to discover an eruption of snow white mushrooms in my garden. An overnight metamorphosis resulted in some giant specimens, inedible unfortunately, but stunning to look at. They appeared in the grass, next to rocks, and in the dark, damp soil by the trees. They looked so tempting and beautiful nestled in the ground that I set about creating an edible version of the scene. I encourage you to dig in!

Serves 8 people

2 cups forbidden rice—rinsed

1/3 cup finely chopped chives

1/3 cup finely chopped parsley

1/2 cup finely sliced green onions

1/4 cup lemon olive oil

1/4 cup lemon juice

Salt

Black pepper

Olive oil

2 tablespoons butter

1 tablespoon butter

1/2 lb cremini mushrooms—cleaned, left whole

1/2 lb beech mushrooms—separated into small clusters

1 Place the rice in a medium saucepan with 3 cups of water and a pinch of salt. Bring to a boil. Reduce heat to low. Cover and cook for 20–25 minutes, or until the rice is tender and the water has been absorbed.

2 Combine the cooked rice, chives, parsley and green onions in a mixing bowl. Sprinkle with some salt and 7–8 grinds of pepper. Add 1/4 cup of olive oil and the lemon juice and mix well. Spread the rice mixture in an even layer on a large platter.

3 Melt the butter with a little olive oil in a large skillet over medium heat. Add the mushrooms, a pinch of salt and some pepper. Cook the mushrooms until golden brown, stirring frequently, approximately 7–8 minutes.

4 Arrange clumps of cooked mushroom in the rice to look like they are growing out of the black "soil." Serve while the mushrooms are still warm.

Grilled Mushroom, Snow Pea and Bok Choy Salad

There is a store near my home that sells an eclectic selection of Anglo-Indo-Chinese foods. Among the 57 varieties of soy sauce, nine brands of basmati rice, countless types of noodles, spices and fish sauces, you'll find English toffees, dozens of tea, Marmite and assorted jams, pickles and chutneys. Tucked in the back of this establishment are refrigerated cases which contain all sorts of exotic vegetables. I had gone there recently to pick up some king trumpet mushrooms for a photo shoot, and, as often happens when I am in an interesting food emporium, I was tempted by other tasty treats including beech mushrooms, bok choy, fresh ginger and snow peas. I also picked up some digestive biscuits and a jar of pickled tamarind leaves. Once home, fortified with a strong cup of tea and one or two of said biscuits, I set about to make this salad—without the tamarind leaves!

Serves 8 people

Olive oil

Juice and zest of 1 lemon

1-inch piece of ginger—
   peeled and finely grated

Salt

Black pepper

3/4 lb snow peas

6 king trumpet mushrooms—
   thinly sliced lengthwise

3/4 lb beech mushrooms—
   separated

8 small bok choy—rinsed
   and quartered

1/4 cup cilantro leaves

1 In a medium salad bowl, whisk together 1/4 cup of olive oil, the lemon juice, zest and grated ginger. Add a pinch of salt and 5–6 grinds of pepper. Place serving utensils over the vinaigrette.

2 Pour a little olive oil into a mixing bowl. Add the snow peas and toss to coat.

3 Heat a grill pan over medium heat. Cook the snow peas for just 1–2 minutes on each side. They cook quickly — be careful not to let them char. Add the cooked peas to the salad bowl on top of the utensils.

4 Add the mushrooms to the mixing bowl, drizzle with a little olive oil and toss to coat. In batches, grill the mushrooms for 3–4 minutes on each side. Add the cooked mushrooms to the salad bowl.

5 Add the bok choy to the mixing bowl and drizzle with a little olive oil. Toss to coat. Grill the bok choy for 3–4 minutes on each side. Add them to the salad bowl.

6 Add the cilantro leaves to the salad bowl and toss all the vegetables to combine well. Serve while the mushrooms are still warm.

Tagliatelle and Chanterelles

There are few things that I find as enjoyable as freshly made pasta. I once spent an afternoon making tagliatelle with my good friend Harriet. It is ridiculously satisfying to pass the dough through the pasta machine and watch it emerge in ribbons on the other side; and I love draping the delicate egg yolk colored strands on the stand to dry. If you don't make your own—I rarely do—and are able to purchase fresh egg noodles, this is the dish to make with them. It is slightly decadent, well no, really quite decadent, but absolutely worth the splurge. Next time I find chanterelles at the market, Harriet and I plan to make this dish together.

Serves 8 people

1 tablespoon olive oil

2 large shallots—peeled and finely sliced

4 tablespoons butter

3 lbs chanterelle mushrooms—carefully cleaned and sliced

Salt

Black pepper

4 oz crème fraîche

¼ cup finely chopped parsley

¼ cup finely chopped chives

1 cup vegetable stock

1 lb tagliatelle (1¼ lbs fresh pasta)

Parmesan cheese for grating (optional)

1 Heat the olive oil in a large pan over medium heat. Add the shallots and cook for 3–4 minutes until just golden brown.

2 Add 3 tablespoons butter, let it melt completely before adding the mushrooms, a pinch of salt and 5–6 grinds of pepper. Cook, stirring frequently, until the mushrooms are golden brown, 7–8 minutes.

3 Gently stir in the crème fraîche, parsley, chives and stock. Keep warm in the pan until ready to serve.

4 Bring a large saucepan of salted water to a rolling boil. Add the pasta, stirring to separate the noodles, and cook until *al dente*. Dried pasta will take about 6–8 minutes; fresh pasta will take only a minute or two. Drain the pasta and return to the saucepan. Add the remaining butter and toss to coat.

5 Divide the pasta among individual warm bowls. Spoon the mushroom mixture on top, grate a little Parmesan and serve immediately.

Mushroom and Asparagus Quiche

Quiche always makes me think of picnics or lunch in the garden. As soon as the warm spring weather arrives, this is the dish I like to make as part of a giant *al fresco* meal for friends and family. It can, of course, be enjoyed indoors; it's up to you.

Serves 8 to 10 people

For the short crust pastry:

9 oz (2 cups) unbleached all-purpose flour

5½ oz butter—cut into small pieces

1 large egg

Zest of 1 lemon

1 tablespoon finely chopped chives

Pinch of salt

For the filling:

Olive oil

4 green onions—thinly sliced

1 lb asparagus—woody ends trimmed, cut into 1-inch pieces

2 tablespoons butter

1 lb assorted mushrooms— thinly sliced

Salt

Black pepper

8 eggs

4 oz grated cheese— Manchego, Gruyère or a variety of cheeses

2 tablespoons crème fraîche

1 Preheat the oven to 400 degrees.

2 Butter a 9-inch wide, 2-inch deep fluted tart pan with a removable bottom.

3 Place all the pastry ingredients in the bowl of a food processor fitted with a metal blade. Pulse until the mixture resembles coarse breadcrumbs. Use longer pulses until the dough forms a ball. Wrap the dough in plastic wrap and refrigerate for 20 minutes.

4 While the dough is resting, prepare the filling. Heat a little oil in a large skillet over medium heat. Cook the green onions for 2–3 minutes, stirring frequently until lightly browned. Add the asparagus and cook for 6–7 minutes. Place in a bowl.

5 Melt 2 tablespoons of butter in the same skillet. Add the mushrooms, a good pinch of salt and 7–8 grinds of pepper, and cook until golden brown, approximately 6–7 minutes. Combine the cooked mushrooms with the asparagus.

6 In a medium mixing bowl, whisk together the eggs, cheese and crème fraîche.

7 On a floured board, roll out the dough to a 14-inch circle. Line the tart pan with the dough. Trim the edges with a sharp knife and prick the dough with a fork. Line the dough with parchment paper and fill with pie weights or dried beans. Bake for 10 minutes until a pale gold color, carefully remove the parchment paper and weights, and bake for 5 more minutes. Remove from the oven and let cool for 5–10 minutes.

8 Fill the quiche shell with the vegetables. Pour the eggs over the vegetables and return to bake in the oven for 20 minutes or until golden brown.

9 To serve, slice the quiche into wedges and serve with a green salad.

PEAS, BEANS & SPROUTS

Fava Smash Crostini
with Buffalo
Mozzarella

—

Spring Pea and Orca
Bean Salad

—

Haricots Verts, Purple
Potato and Smoked
Salmon Salad

—

Grilled Baby Gem and
Snap Pea Salad

—

Multi-Colored
Haricots Verts Salad

—

Sprouted Pea and
Raw Peanut Salad

—

Seared Ahi with
Spring Peas and
Sprouts

—

Spring Pea, Fava
Bean and Roasted
Tomato Tart

Fava Smash Crostini with Buffalo Mozzarella

I often make myself a toasted avocado sandwich for lunch. This takes that buttery treat to a different level of lusciousness. I would quite happily eat these for breakfast, lunch and dinner.

Serves 8 as an appetizer

2 lbs fava beans

Olive oil

Salt

Black pepper

2 tablespoons finely chopped basil

1 tablespoon finely chopped mint

1 tablespoon finely chopped chives

8 slices olive bread—toasted

Lemon olive oil

1 buffalo mozzarella—sliced

4 slices prosciutto

2 ripe avocados—halved, peeled and sliced

2 lemons—quartered

1 Shell the fava beans. Slit open the pods and remove the beans. Boil them in heavily salted water for 1 minute. Drain and immediately plunge the beans into a bowl of ice water to stop the cooking and set the bright color. Tear the tough skin at the rounded end and squeeze out the bean.

2 Heat a little olive in a medium pan. Add the shelled fava beans, a pinch of salt and 4–5 grinds of pepper, and cook for 3–4 minutes. They should be fork tender but not mushy. Place the fava beans in a mixing bowl and drizzle with a little more olive oil. Roughly mash the beans with a fork.

3 Add the basil, mint and chives and mix well.

4 Drizzle a little lemon olive oil over each toast. Place the sliced mozzarella on top.

5 Cover 4 toasts with a slice of mozzarella, a slice of prosciutto and some sliced avocado.

6 Cover the remaining toasts with a slice of mozzarella and some sliced avocado.

7 Spoon the fava beans over each toast. Sprinkle with a little salt and pepper. Serve with lemon wedges to squeeze over the toasts.

Spring Pea and Orca Bean Salad

This dish is a little like my family, half French and half English—a combination that can be fraught with difficulties in many aspects of life, most notably in the kitchen. The French side serves peas and other legumes with a vinaigrette; the English side serves peas with mint. I thought I would try the two together—a culinary Entente Cordiale of sorts—and see if they fared well. They do, thankfully, just like my family!

Serves 8 people

For the salad:

1¼ cup unshelled or ½ cup shelled fava beans

2 cups orca beans

Olive oil

2 shallots—peeled and thinly sliced

2 cups uncooked shelled green peas

Juice of 1 lemon

½ cup packed mint leaves—roughly chopped

For the vinaigrette:

1 tablespoon Dijon mustard

¼ cup olive oil

2 tablespoons lemon juice

1 tablespoon white wine vinegar or Champagne vinegar

Pinch of salt

4–5 grinds black pepper

1 Shell the fava beans. Slit open the pods and remove the beans. Boil them in heavily salted water for 1 minute. Drain and immediately plunge the beans into a bowl of ice water to stop the cooking and set the bright color. Tear the tough skin at the rounded end and squeeze out the bean.

2 Place the orca beans in a large saucepan with 4 cups of cold water. Cover and bring to a boil. Reduce heat to medium-low and cook until tender, about 50–60 minutes. Make sure the beans are completely covered with water during cooking. Add more water if necessary. Drain and rinse under cold water.

3 Heat a little olive oil in a medium saucepan. Sauté the shallots until golden brown, about 4–5 minutes. Add the green peas and shelled fava beans and cook for 3 minutes. Add the cooked orca beans and lemon juice, and gently mix to combine. Remove from the heat.

4 In a medium salad bowl, whisk together all the vinaigrette ingredients to form a thick emulsion. Add the beans and peas to the bowl and toss well to coat. Add the mint leaves just before serving.

Haricots Verts, Purple Potato and Smoked Salmon Salad

As a young child, one of my favorite pastimes when I visited my grandmother's home, was to leaf through her collection of books on Impressionist art. The grand books were housed in cream colored slipcases embossed with the artist's name. Together, we would carefully turn the pages and she would ask me questions about what I saw. I particularly liked Matisse and Cezanne, the vitality of their paintings, and the manner in which they combined color. I often approach plating food in the same way, appealing to the visual senses first. When I first made this dish, it made me think of Matisse's still life paintings filled with vibrant ochre, emerald greens and purple hues— a colorful play on a Salade Niçoise.

Serves 8 people

For the salad:

3/4 lb haricots verts—
    ends trimmed

Juice of 1 lemon

1 lb purple potatoes

Salt

Olive oil

2 shallots—peeled
    and finely diced

2 green onions—
    finely sliced

Black pepper

1/4 lb uncooked shelled
    green peas

2 Belgian endives—
    thinly sliced

8 oz smoked salmon

For the vinaigrette:

1/4 cup olive oil

Juice and zest of 1 lemon

2 tablespoons finely
    chopped chives

1 Steam the haricots verts until just tender, about 5–6 minutes. Remove from the steamer and rinse under cold water. Place in a bowl and toss with the lemon juice.

2 Fill a large saucepan with cold water. Add the potatoes and a good pinch of salt. Bring to a boil, then reduce to a steady simmer. Cook until a paring knife easily pierces the potatoes, 20 to 25 minutes. Drain and let rest until cool enough to handle. Peel the potatoes, then cut into 1/4-inch slices.

3 Heat a little olive oil in a medium saucepan. Add the shallots and cook until lightly golden, about 3–4 minutes. Add the green onions, a pinch of salt, 5–6 grinds of pepper and the green peas. Cook 1–2 minutes.

4 In a medium salad bowl, vigorously whisk together all the vinaigrette ingredients to form an emulsion. Add all the vegetables and smoked salmon and toss gently.

Grilled Baby Gem and Snap Pea Salad with Pistachio Herb Pesto

One of my favorite local farmers is a man named Jacob Grant. In 2002, he started Roots Organic Farm in the little California town of Los Olivos. Chefs and locals regularly swarm his market stand, clamoring for his fresh, vibrant fruits and vegetables. He sells, amongst other things, four varieties of baby gem lettuces. Baby gems, a small form of romaine, are crisp, crunchy and sweet. They lend themselves well to all manner of preparations: left raw and gently torn for a salad, sautéed, braised or grilled. I particularly like the latter, as grilling the vegetable brings out its herbaceous flavor and is delightful when combined with peas. Making this salad with such vibrant ingredients is a spring and summertime pleasure.

Serves 8 people

1 cup parsley leaves

1/2 cup mint leaves

1/4 cup pistachios

2 tablespoons chopped chives

Zest and juice of 1 lemon

Olive oil

4 baby gem lettuces—outer leaves removed, quartered lengthwise

1 lb sugar snap peas—cut diagonally

Salt

Black pepper

1 In a food processor fitted with the metal blade, chop the parsley, mint, pistachios and chives using short pulses. Add the lemon juice and zest. With the machine running, pour in the olive oil and process until the pesto is fairly smooth.

2 Heat a grill pan over medium high heat.

3 Place the baby gems into a medium mixing bowl and drizzle with a little olive oil. Toss to coat. Grill the baby gems for just 1–2 minutes per side. They cook quickly—be careful not to char them. Place the grilled lettuce onto a serving platter.

4 Place the snap peas into a mixing bowl. Drizzle with a little olive oil, a good pinch of salt and 7–8 grinds of pepper. Grill the snap peas for 2–3 minutes, turning them once or twice.

5 Scatter the grilled snap peas over and around the baby gems. Spoon the pesto over the vegetables. Serve warm.

Haricots Verts and Roasted Carrot Salad

Salad of haricots verts, the thin French variety of green beans, is a favorite of mine, and I like to make variations by building on the classic foundation of steamed beans, shallots and a mustard vinaigrette. In this lovely, bright, spring salad, I have added colorful roasted carrots, fragrant whole basil leaves and zingy lemon zest. You can also add some savory granola for a crunchy topping.

Serves 8 people

1 lb red carrots—peeled, quartered lengthwise, cut in 4-inch sticks

5–6 green onions—sliced

2 shallots—peeled and finely sliced

Olive oil

Salt and black pepper

1 lb haricots verts—trimmed

1 tablespoon Dijon mustard

1/4 cup olive oil

1 tablespoon white wine vinegar or tarragon vinegar

1/4 cup finely chopped chives

Zest of 1 lemon

1/2 cup loosely packed basil leaves

2 tablespoons savory granola (page 208, optional)

1 Preheat the oven to 375 degrees.

2 Place the carrots, green onions and shallots on a rimmed sheet pan. Drizzle with a little olive oil and toss to coat. Season with salt and pepper. Roast for 15 minutes.

3 While the carrots are roasting, steam the haricots verts until *al dente*, about 5–7 minutes. Remove them from the steamer and blanch in ice water to stop the cooking and set the bright color. Drain.

4 In a large bowl, vigorously whisk together the mustard, vinegar and olive oil to create an emulsion. Add the cooked carrots, haricots verts and chives and toss to coat.

5 Place the dressed vegetables on a large serving platter and finish the salad by scattering the lemon zest and basil leaves on top. For added texture and flavor, sprinkle with 2 tablespoons of savory granola.

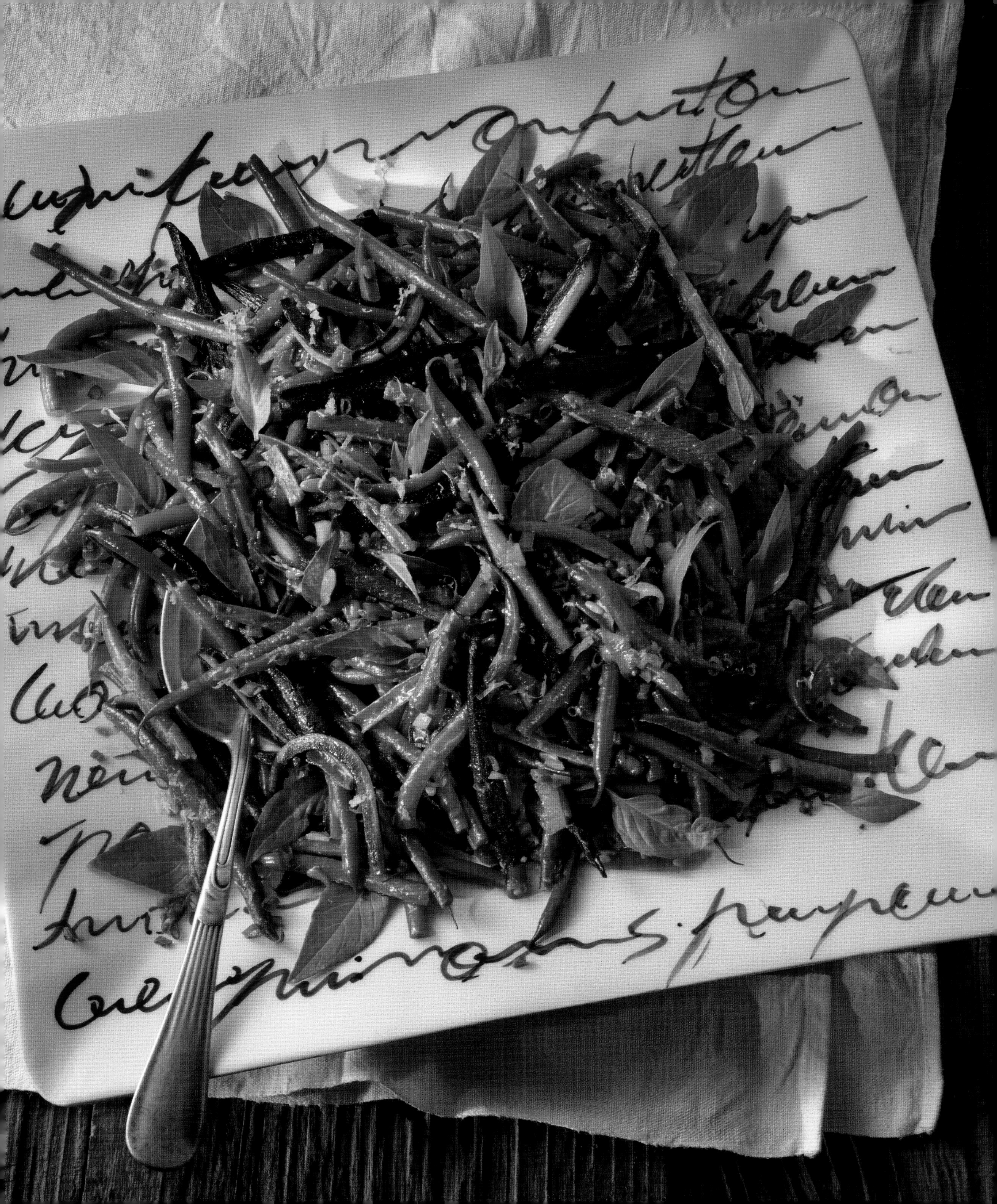

Sprouted Pea and Raw Peanut Salad with Lemon Ginger Vinaigrette

For the past 15 years, I have been buying mixed sprouts from the same farm stand at my local market. The ladies at Ojai Valley Sprouts grow an abundant variety of organic sprouts including pea greens, red rose radish, spicy arugula, onion sprouts, sprouted lentils, peas and peanuts. I like to eat the raw, sprouted peanuts by the handful and had been thinking about new ways to incorporate them into my cooking, when, on a recent visit, I spied them beside the black—eyed and sprouted peas. Ooh, what about a multi-pea-bean-peanut concoction with a spicy vinaigrette? I bought some lemongrass, ginger, basil and snow peas from a Laotian farmer at the same market, and dashed home to make this salad.

Serves 8 people

2 cups sprouted
   black-eyed peas

2 cups sprouted peas

Salt

2 tablespoons olive oil

1 tablespoon peanut oil

1 stalk lemon grass—split
   and cut into 2-inch pieces

1 yellow or white onion—
   finely sliced

3-4 green onions—finely
   sliced

1-inch piece ginger—peeled
   and minced

1 cup sprouted peanuts

½ lb snow peas

Juice and zest of 1 lemon

Juice and zest of 1 lime

1 packed cup basil leaves—
   roughly torn

Black pepper

1. Place the black-eyed peas in a large saucepan of lightly salted water and bring to a boil. Reduce to a simmer and cook for 20 minutes. Add the sprouted peas to the saucepan and cook for 10 minutes. Drain thoroughly.

2. While the peas are cooking, prepare the rest of the salad. Heat the olive and peanut oils in a large skillet. Add the lemongrass pieces, onion, green onions and ginger and cook until just golden brown, about 2-3 minutes. Add the peanuts and snow peas, and cook for 1-2 minutes. Remove from the heat. Discard the lemongrass pieces. Stir in the lemon and lime zests and juice, a good pinch of salt and 6-7 grinds of pepper. Transfer the vegetables into a medium salad or serving bowl.

3. Add the cooked peas and basil leaves. Toss gently to combine. Serve warm.

Seared Ahi with Spring Peas and Sprouts

Eating raw fish is not something I ever did before I moved to California. I vividly remember my first visit to a sushi bar. I started timidly at first, with the easy, ubiquitous California roll, and then a hand roll before becoming more adventurous and trying nigiri, different types of sashimi, and barely seared ahi. That was a revelation! I loved the ocean freshness of the raw and nearly raw fish. I then tried my hand at making sushi at home. Some of my creations were more successful than others! Now when I splurge on some super fresh ahi, I like to prepare it with that briefest of sears and serve it on a vibrant green bed of sautéed vegetables.

Serves 8 people

For the marinade and ahi:

1 tablespoon olive oil

1 teaspoon soy sauce

1 teaspoon honey

1 teaspoon finely chopped fresh *za'atar* leaves or finely chopped fresh oregano

Large pinch of salt

Black pepper

2¹/₂ lbs ahi tuna

For the vegetables:

1 lb haricots verts— ends trimmed

Olive oil

2 red onions— peeled, quartered and thinly sliced

¹/₂ lb snap peas—sliced lengthwise on a bias

3 cups packed baby spinach leaves

3 cups pea sprouts

Juice of 2 limes

Salt

Black pepper

1 In a small bowl, whisk together the oil, soy sauce, honey, *za'atar*, salt and 6–7 grinds of pepper. Place the ahi in a shallow dish. Pour the marinade over the ahi and turn to coat thoroughly. Marinate the ahi for 30 minutes.

2 Steam the haricots verts until *al dente*, about 6–7 minutes. Remove from the steamer.

3 Heat a little olive oil in a large skillet. Sauté the onions, stirring frequently until lightly golden, about 5–6 minutes. Add the snap peas and cook for 3–4 minutes. Add the spinach and cook until just wilted, about 1–2 minutes. Mix in the sprouts and cook 1–2 minutes. Add the lime juice, a good pinch of salt and pepper. Reduce the heat to very low.

4 Heat a grill pan over medium high heat. Sear the ahi for about 1¹/₂ minutes on each side. Be careful not to overcook it, otherwise it will be dry. Place the seared ahi on a cutting board and slice into ³/₄-inch thick pieces. Place the pieces on top of the cooked vegetables and serve immediately.

Spring Pea, Fava Bean and Roasted Tomato Tart

Whilst going through a stack of food magazines, I came across a photograph of a stunning berry tart whose center had been cut out—the tart that is, not the photograph. I love tarts and decided to make a savory version in the same wreath shape. I love the touch of whimsy.

Serves 8 to 10 people

For the tart shell:

9 oz (2 cups) unbleached all-purpose flour

5½ oz (11 tablespoons) butter—chilled, cut into small pieces

Zest of 1 lemon

1 large egg

Pinch of salt

For the filling:

½ pint cherry tomatoes

Olive oil

Salt

Black pepper

2 teaspoons *herbes de Provence*

1 lb fava beans

2 shallots—peeled, halved and thinly sliced

½ lb snap peas— cut on a bias

½ lb shelled English peas

½ cup Greek yogurt

2 oz feta cheese cheese— crumbled

½ cup ricotta cheese

1 tablespoon finely chopped chives

½ cup small mint leaves

1. Preheat the oven to 400 degrees, and butter a 12-inch tart pan with a removable bottom.

2. Pulse all the tart shell ingredients in the bowl of a food processor until the mixture resembles coarse breadcrumbs. Use longer pulses until the dough forms a ball. Wrap the dough in plastic wrap and refrigerate for 20 minutes. (You can make the dough ahead of time and remove it from the fridge 20 minutes before using.)

3. On a lightly floured board, roll out the dough to a 14-inch circle. Line the tart pan with the dough, trim the edges with a sharp knife, and then prick the dough with a fork. Cut a hole in the center by running a sharp knife around the edge of a water glass. Remove the circle of dough and reserve for another use. Line the dough with parchment paper and fill with pie weights or dried beans.

4. Bake the tart shell for 15 minutes. Carefully remove the parchment paper and weights. Return the tart to the oven and bake until golden brown, about 10 minutes. Let cool on a wire rack.

5. Place the cherry tomatoes in a small baking dish. Drizzle to coat with olive oil, add a pinch of salt, a little pepper and the *herbes de Provence*. Roast for 30 minutes. Remove from the oven and leave in the pan.

6. Prepare the fava beans. Slit open the pods and remove the beans. Boil them in heavily salted water for 1 minute. Drain and immediately plunge the beans into a bowl of ice water to stop the cooking and set the bright color. Tear the tough skin at the rounded end and squeeze out the bean.

7. In a large skillet, sauté the shallots for 3–4 minutes in a little olive oil. Add the snap peas, a pinch of salt and some pepper and cook for 2–3 minutes. Finally, add the fava beans and English peas and cook 2 minutes. Remove from the heat.

8. In a small bowl, using a fork, mix together the yogurt, feta, ricotta, pinch of salt, pepper and chives.

9. Place the tart shell on a platter. Spread the bottom of the tart with the yogurt-feta mixture. Layer the pea-fava bean mixture on top. Dot with the tomatoes and tuck the mint leaves in amongst the peas. Serve warm.

POTATOES & ROOT VEGETABLES

Smoked Salmon and
Potato Delights

~

Potato, Dill and
Shallot Salad

~

Roasted Parsnip and
Arugula Salad

~

Roasted Fingerlings
Stuffed with Pesto

~

Mashed Spuds with
Crème Fraîche

~

Sweet Potato Fries

~

Roasted Parsnips with
Moroccan Spices

~

Potato and
Celeriac Gratin

~

Root Vegetable Roast

Smoked Salmon Potato Delights

I often serve little smoked salmon toasts as an appetizer for dinner parties, but sometimes I like to make something a little extra special—these potato delights are just that. They're crispy on the outside, soft on the inside and topped with tangy crème fraîche that complements the smoked salmon. These are marvelous served with a glass of bubbly!

Serves 8 people as an appetizer

2 lbs russet potatoes

Olive oil

Salt

Black pepper

1/2 cup crème fraîche

2 tablespoons lemon juice

1/3 cup finely chopped chives

8 oz smoked salmon

2 oz salmon roe

1 Preheat the oven to 450 degrees.

2 Peel and coarsely grate the potatoes. Don't worry if they begin to change color.

3 Pour a liberal dose of olive oil onto a rimmed sheet pan. To form a potato disk, place two heaped tablespoons of the grated potatoes onto the baking pan. Use a spatula to flatten it into a disk about 3 inches wide. Make a total of 16 disks. Sprinkle with salt and pepper.

4 Bake the potato disks for 8 minutes. Carefully flip the disks, press them lightly and continue baking 6–8 minutes, or until golden brown. Remove from the oven and place them on a paper towel.

5 In a small bowl, mix the crème fraîche, lemon juice and all but one tablespoon of the chives.

6 Place the potato disks on a serving platter. Spoon a little of the crème fraîche mixture onto each disk. Top with some smoked salmon, a little salmon roe and a sprinkling of chopped chives. Serve warm.

Potato, Dill and Shallot Salad

The key to this salad is using fingerling potatoes—if available, a mix of yellow, red and purple ones. The varieties have marvelous names such as Purple Congo, Desiree, Golden Wonder, Roosevelt and Jaune de Holland. I first fell in love with these buttery, tasty tubers in France and in England where they were plentiful at our local green grocer. Years later, I found them at the local markets here in California where they are now as plentiful and just as delicious. They are my favorite potato.

Serves 8 as a side dish

2 lbs small fingerling
   potatoes

1/4 cup extra virgin olive oil

1/4 cup Greek yogurt

Zest and juice of 1 lemon

2 shallots—peeled and
   finely diced

1/4 cup finely chopped dill

2 tablespoons finely
   chopped chives

Pinch coarse sea salt

5-6 grinds black pepper

1. Steam the potatoes until they are fork tender, about 15-20 minutes. Remove from the steamer and let cool for 5 minutes before assembling the salad.

2. In a medium salad bowl, whisk together all the remaining ingredients. Add the potatoes to the bowl and toss to coat well. Serve at room temperature.

Roasted Parsnip and Arugula Salad

Roasted parsnips have a sweet, earthy flavor and are the perfect foil for light leafed, peppery arugula. This is a great salad to serve with some Portobello mushrooms, roast chicken or crispy duck.

Serves 8 people

1½ lbs parsnips—
    peeled, cut into
    ½ x ½-inch sticks

Olive oil

Coarse sea salt

Black pepper

1 tablespoon Dijon or walnut
    mustard

2 tablespoons olive oil

1 tablespoon almond oil

1 tablespoon white wine
    vinegar

8 oz baby arugula

2 Belgian endives—ends
    trimmed, thinly sliced

½ cup almonds—roughly
    chopped

12 large dates—chopped

1 Preheat the oven to 375 degrees.

2 Place the sliced parsnips in a large mixing bowl. Drizzle with a little olive oil and toss to coat. Place the parsnips on a rimmed sheet pan. Sprinkle with a little salt and add 6–7 grinds of pepper. Roast in the middle of the oven for 30 minutes, turning the parsnips halfway through the cooking time. Remove from the oven and let cool for 5 minutes.

3 While the parsnips are roasting, prepare the vinaigrette. In a large salad bowl, whisk together the mustard, olive and almond oils and the vinegar to form an emulsion. Place serving utensils over the vinaigrette.

4 Place the arugula, endives, almonds and dates on top of the salad utensils. Add the cooked parsnips. When ready to serve, toss the salad well. This salad is best served while the parsnips are still warm.

Roasted Fingerlings Stuffed with Pesto

This dish combines two of my favorite foods—fingerling potatoes and pesto. I love to find the first spring potatoes at the market and experiment with different preparations. This one is quick and easy to make. The dish pairs well with green salads, haricots verts and roasted kale.

Serves 8 people as a side dish

For the potatoes:

2 lbs fingerling potatoes

Olive oil

Salt

Black pepper

2 oz feta cheese—crumbled

For the pesto:

2 cups packed basil leaves

1 cup parsley leaves

1 cup cilantro leaves

1/3 cup grated Parmesan cheese

1/3 cup toasted pine nuts

1/2 cup olive oil

1 Preheat the oven to 375 degrees.

2 Place the potatoes on a shallow baking tray. Drizzle with a little olive oil, sprinkle with a little salt and add 6–7 grinds of pepper. Roast the potatoes until they are golden and fork tender, about 30 minutes.

3 While the potatoes are roasting, prepare the pesto. Place the basil, parsley and cilantro leaves into a food processor. Pulse until the herbs are finely chopped. Add the Parmesan and pine nuts. Pulse a few times more to combine the ingredients. With the machine running, pour in the olive oil and process until well blended but still moderately coarse.

4 Slice open each potato lengthwise. Do not slice all the way through. Spoon some pesto into each potato and dot with the crumbled feta. Serve hot.

Mashed Spuds with Crème Fraîche

There are few things more delicious than a bowl of silky mashed potatoes. The key to good creamy potatoes is the ratio of butter to cream to spud. I have been fortunate enough to have tasted the legendary potatoes prepared by chefs Michel Richard and Joël Robuchon, who use prodigious quantities of butter to transform this humble dish into an ethereal, if not potentially heart-stopping, concoction. My version is not quite as rich, but it is luscious and velvety—just as mashed spuds should be.

Serves 8 people as a side dish

2 lbs Yukon golds or russets—
    peeled and cubed

Coarse sea salt

7 oz butter—softened

1 cup milk

4 oz crème fraîche

1   Place the potatoes in a large saucepan of salted, cold water. Bring to a boil, then reduce to a strong simmer. Cook the potatoes until they are fork tender. Drain the potatoes, return them to the saucepan and let them release their steam for 1–2 minutes. Transfer them to a large bowl.

2   Pass the potatoes through a ricer and return them to the saucepan. Add the butter, milk and crème fraîche and stir until fully incorporated and the potatoes are fluffy and creamy. Season to taste. Serve immediately.

Sweet Potato Fries

Every now and then, my lovely mum and I go out to a local tapas bar for dinner. Being creatures of habit, we always order their sweet potato fries. I decided to surprise my mum when she came to dinner at my house one night, by making my own fries — with a little Provençale twist. They were a hit! I like to serve them with assorted salads and some tzatziki.

Serves 8 people as a side dish

2 large sweet potatoes—
    peeled, cut into
    3/8 x 3/8-inch sticks

Olive oil

1½ tablespoons *herbes de Provence*

Large pinch of coarse sea salt

7–8 grinds black pepper

1   Preheat the oven to 375 degrees.

2   Place the sweet potatoes in a mixing bowl. Drizzle with olive oil, add the *herbes de Provence* and toss to coat well. Place the potatoes, widely spaced, on a rimmed sheet pan. Do not crowd them or they will become limp. Use a second sheet pan if necessary. Sprinkle with salt and pepper.

3   Bake for 20 minutes. Turn the sweet potatoes, increase the temperature to 400 degrees and bake for an additional 10–15 minutes. The fries are ready when they are lightly browned. Serve immediately.

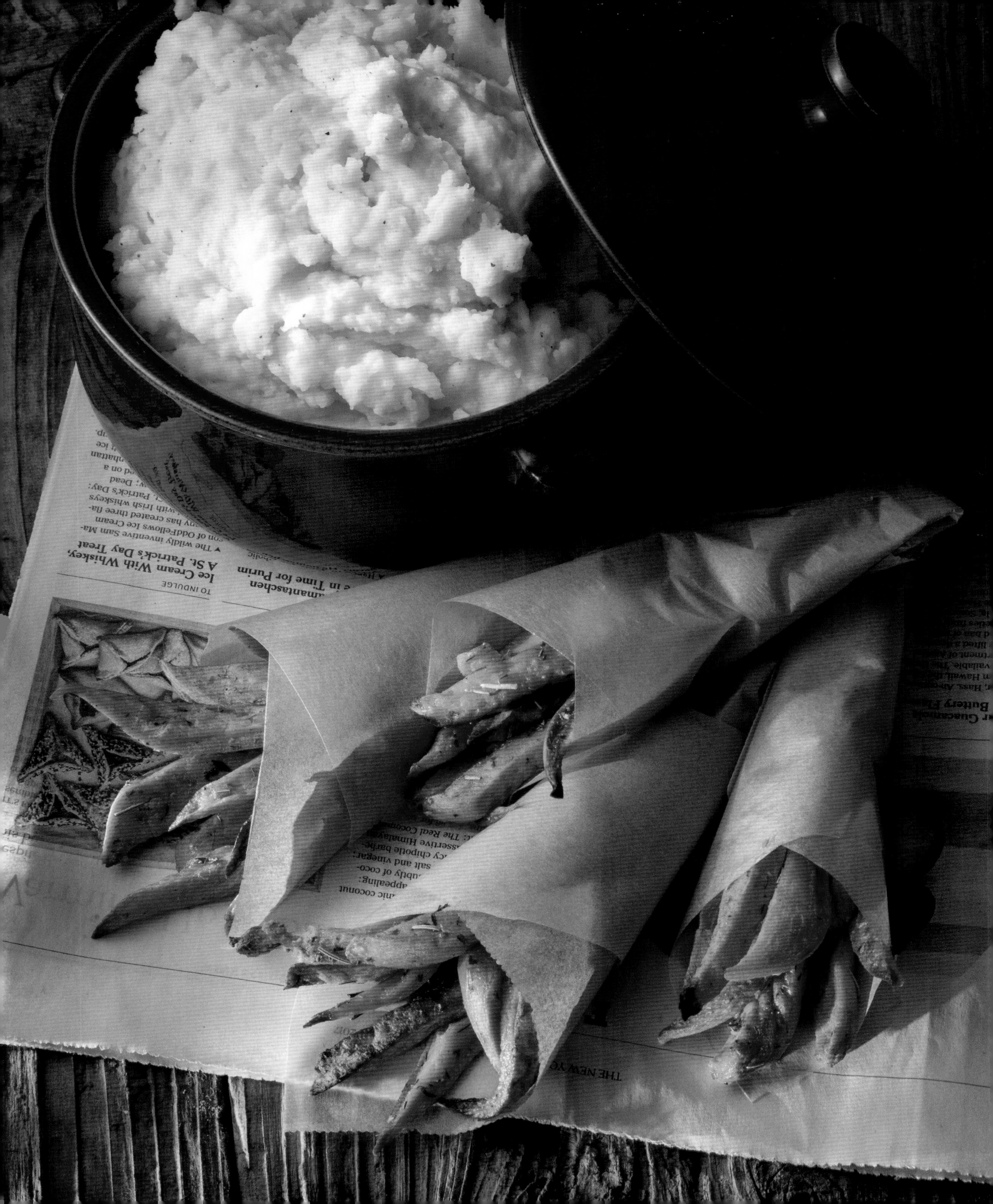

Roasted Parsnips with Moroccan Spices

The fragrant spices in the *ras el hanout* perfume this dish, infuse the parsnips, Jerusalem artichokes and onions with a little heat, and give the vegetables a pale golden hue. This spice mix is a staple in North African kitchens, particularly in Morocco where it is said to originate. The name means "best of the house" and the mixture contains anywhere from one to two dozen spices. The exact blend is unique to each kitchen. I think that is part of what makes *ras el hanout* so alluring. It's a spice mixture that will tickle your olfactory senses!

Serves 8 people

For the vegetables:

2 lbs parsnips—peeled, cut into ⅜ x ⅜-inch sticks

1 lb Jerusalem artichokes—peeled and sliced

2 large red onions—peeled, halved and thinly sliced

Olive oil

Salt

1 tablespoon *ras el hanout*

½ cup golden raisins

½ cup almonds—chopped

Cilantro leaves for garnish

For the yogurt sauce:

1 cup Greek yogurt

2 tablespoons finely chopped cilantro

2 tablespoons finely chopped chives

Zest and juice of 1 lemon

1. Preheat the oven to 375 degrees.

2. Place the parsnips, Jerusalem artichokes and red onions in a large mixing bowl. Drizzle with olive oil, a good pinch of salt and the *ras el hanout*. Toss to coat well. Place the vegetables on a rimmed sheet pan or in a shallow baking dish. Roast for 30 minutes or until golden brown, turning the vegetables once or twice.

3. While the vegetables are roasting, prepare the yogurt sauce. In a small bowl, whisk together all the ingredients. Let rest at room temperature.

4. As soon as the vegetables come out of the oven, add the golden raisins and almonds, and mix well. Transfer to a serving dish and dot with cilantro leaves. Serve with the yogurt sauce.

Potato and Celeriac Gratin

A potato gratin is always a pretty decadent dish. In this version, potatoes are combined with celeriac, bathed in an unctuous mixture of cream and crème fraîche, and baked until all its cheesy goodness is golden brown. So yummy!

Serves 8 people

8 oz crème fraîche

1½ cups cream

Salt

Black pepper

2 lbs potatoes (russets or Yukon golds)— peeled, very thinly sliced on a mandolin

2 lbs celeriac (celery root)— peeled, very thinly sliced on a mandolin

3 tablespoons finely chopped chives

3-4 green onions— finely sliced

4 oz Gruyère cheese— grated

1 Preheat the oven to 375 degrees.

2 In a large bowl, whisk together the crème fraîche and cream. Add a good pinch of salt and 5-6 grinds of pepper and whisk once more.

3 Add the remaining ingredients to the bowl and mix well. The easiest way to do this is with your hands. It's a little messy, but fun!

4 Layer the well-coated potatoes and celeriac slices in a large gratin dish or individual gratins, slightly overlapping them.

5 Bake for 35-40 minutes or until the vegetables are tender and the top of the gratin is golden brown. Remove from the oven and let rest for 5 minutes before serving.

Root Vegetable Roast

This is one of my favorite, everyday vegetable meals. I chop up whatever root veggies I have on hand, drizzle them with a good hearty olive oil, and pop them in the oven. It is a very versatile dish and changes with the seasons. I sometimes top it with a little goat cheese or perhaps a vibrant pesto, and usually serve it with a large green salad.

Serves 8 people

1 lb assorted baby potatoes—
    halved

1/2 lb parsnips—peeled,
    cut lengthwise into
    1/2-inch pieces

1 1/2 lbs carrots (a mix of
    yellow, orange and red)—
    peeled, cut lengthwise
    into 1/2-inch sticks

1 lb Jerusalem artichokes—
    peeled and sliced

2 small celery root—peeled,
    quartered and sliced

1 bunch parsley root (optional)—
    peeled and sliced

6-7 sprigs fresh thyme

4-5 sprigs fresh oregano

Olive oil

Coarse sea salt

Black pepper

1 Preheat the oven to 350 degrees.

2 Place all the vegetables and herbs in a large shallow baking dish. Drizzle with olive oil and toss to coat well. Sprinkle with salt and pepper. Roast in the center of the oven until golden brown, about 40-45 minutes, turning the vegetables two or three times.

NOTE: This is a wonderful dish to serve as part of a vegetarian dinner or as an accompaniment to any roast.

TOMATOES

Tomato and Avocado Flowers

—

Green Tomato, Melon
and Cucumber Soup

—

Heirloom Tomato
and Burrata Salad with
Savory Granola

—

Bruschetta with
Tomatoes and Figs

—

Toma-Toma

—

Green Tomato,
Green Fig, Goat Cheese
and Mint Salad

—

Club 55 Crudités Salad

—

Tarte aux Tomates

—

Roasted Black Cod and
Saffron-Tomato Sauce

—

Tomato and
Lentils du Puy Curry

—

Tomato and Lemon
Wrapped Roasted Halibut

Tomato and Avocado Flowers

This dish was inspired whilst I was flying across the Atlantic. Unable to sleep and two movies into my flight, I decided to watch a documentary on Louis Comfort Tiffany to while away the last couple of hours of the interminable flight. I was entranced by his use of color and stones to create flowers and birds in his lamps, stained glass windows and jewelry. I started doodling in my recipe sketchbook and came up with these "flowers." I made this as soon as I landed—an edible homage to Tiffany.

Serves 8 people as an appetizer

2 small ripe avocados—
 halved, pitted and peeled

24 chives

24 cherry tomatoes—
 different varieties,
 if available

24 cilantro leaves

1 tablespoon Dijon mustard

3 tablespoons olive oil

1 tablespoon white wine
 vinegar

1 Slice each avocado half vertically, for a total of 8 slices.

2 Arrange the avocado slices on a large serving platter.

3 Insert 3 chive stems into the center of each avocado slice.

4 Partially cross cut each cherry tomato to create a flower. Place a cherry tomato flower at the end of each chive.

5 Add cilantro leaves to either side of the chives. In a small bowl, whisk together the Dijon mustard, olive oil and vinegar to form an emulsion. Put a spoonful of the vinaigrette into the center of each avocado slice.

6 To serve, use a thin spatula to carefully transfer avocado sections to individual salad plates.

Green Tomato, Melon and Cucumber Soup

Last summer was boiling hot, as in too-hot-to-even-think-about-cooking hot. We ate gardens of salads and drank gallons of very cold drinks. One sweltering Saturday morning at the market, I sampled green melons that were so fresh and flavorful that I thought I would try making a chilled soup with them. This was the refreshing result—perfect for a summer's day, boiling or otherwise.

Serves 8 people

For the soup:

1 lb (6–7) green tomatoes

1 green honeydew or Bailan melon (3–3½ lbs)— halved, seeded, peeled and roughly chopped

3 Persian or 1 English cucumber—peeled and roughly chopped

4 tablespoons olive oil

Large pinch of sea salt

5–6 grinds black pepper

For the garnish:

16 yellow pear or small yellow blush tomatoes— quartered

2 tablespoons roughly chopped cilantro leaves

2 tablespoons chopped Thai basil leaves

Zest and juice of 1 lemon

1 tablespoon olive oil

Pinch of coarse sea salt

6–7 grinds black pepper

Pink flake salt

1 Place all the soup ingredients in a blender and purée until smooth. Alternatively, place the ingredients in a deep bowl and purée with an immersion blender. Chill the soup for a minimum of 1 hour.

2 15 minutes before serving the soup, combine all the garnish ingredients in a medium bowl and toss well to combine.

3 Ladle the soup into eight bowls. Spoon some of the garnish into the center of each soup bowl and sprinkle with a little pink flake salt just before serving.

Heirloom Tomato and Burrata Salad with Savory Granola.

I usually start the day with a bowl of Greek yogurt, some berries and homemade granola. When I found myself with an abundance of cherry tomatoes in my kitchen one day, I thought I'd try making a savory version of the granola recipe in my book, Les Fruits. I substituted tomatoes for the berries, the burrata in place of the yogurt, and then there was the combination dry ingredients to figure out. Three batches, many nuts and spices, and a few hours later, I was happy with my mix. This is a fun, unusual dish, and the granola is a treat sprinkled on top of a salad, roasted fish or grilled vegetables (see page 176).

Serves 8 people

For the granola:

2 cups rolled oats

½ cup raw almonds—chopped

⅓ cup flax seed

¼ cup *herbes de Provence*

1 tablespoon *herbes de poisson*—
  or an equal mix of fennel
  seeds, mustard seeds and
  coriander seeds

1 teaspoon salt

¼ cup canola or grapeseed oil

½ cup pistachios

¼ cup pine nuts

½ cup golden raisins

For the burrata:

1 burrata

¼ cup Greek yogurt

Zest and juice of 1 lemon

Coarse sea salt

¼ cup olive oil

Freshly ground pepper

For the tomatoes:

1½ lbs baby heirloom and
  cherry tomatoes—halved

1 tablespoon olive oil

1 large pinch salt

½ cup purple basil leaves—
  finely chopped

1 tablespoon finely chopped
  chives

1 Preheat the oven to 350 degrees.

2 To make the granola, in a large bowl combine the oats, almonds, flax seed, *herbes de Provence*, *herbes de poisson* and salt. Add the oil and mix well.

3 Spread the mixture in an even layer onto a rimmed baking sheet. Bake in the center of the oven for 20 minutes.

4 Add the pistachios and pine nuts to the oats, stir to combine and spread in an even layer once more. Continue to bake for 5 minutes, or until the oats and nuts are golden brown.

5 Remove from the oven and let the granola cool completely before adding the golden raisins. Mix well and store in an airtight container.

6 For the burrata, place all of the ingredients in the bowl of a food processor fitted with a metal blade. Pulse until smooth. Alternatively, use an immersion blender. Spoon the burrata mixture into 8 bowls or glass jars.

7 Put all of the tomato ingredients in a medium bowl and toss well to combine. Divide the tomato mixture and spoon over the burrata in each bowl. Sprinkle with the granola and serve immediately.

Bruschetta with Tomatoes and Figs

Everyone who knows me well, knows that I LOVE figs. Fig jam, fig compotes, figs in salads, figs on salmon, figs with chicken and, well, figs on just about anything. I particularly like how figs and tomatoes complement each other well and are especially mouthwatering on these super quick-to-prepare, sweet-savory bruschetta.

Serves 8 people as an appetizer

8 medium tomatoes (assorted varieties)—diced

4-6 assorted figs—roughly chopped

4 green onions—ends trimmed, finely sliced

2 tablespoons finely chopped chives

2 tablespoons olive oil

2 tablespoons finely chopped basil

Zest of 1 lemon

Zest of 1 lime

8 large or 16 small slices of baguette or olive bread—toasted

Black pepper

1 In a medium bowl, combine the tomatoes, figs, green onions, chives, olive oil, basil and the lemon and lime zest. Toss to coat well.

2 Place the toasts on a serving platter. Spoon the tomato-fig mixture on top and grind some fresh pepper on each bruschetta. Serve immediately.

Toma-Toma

I admit that I adore cookery books, so much so that they now spill off the shelves in my office and stand in delicious stacks on the floor. I spend hours reading them like novels, gobbling up one mouthwatering chapter after another. My favorite books are full of paper scraps marking recipes I want to make, a photo I find inspiring, or perhaps a technique that intrigues me. This dish came about because of a stunning image of peeled, glistening, glazed plums in one of Donna Hays' books. The texture of the plums reminded me of peeled tomatoes so I experimented with different varieties to achieve the same look. The cherry tomatoes worked perfectly and resembled little gems. This dish does take a little extra prep time, but it is not complicated and the result is as pretty as a picture, with the added bonus that you can eat it, too!

Serves 8 people

For the tomato juice:

1¼ lbs yellow heirloom tomatoes—halved

1½ tablespoons basil olive oil

Juice of 1 lemon

Coarse sea salt

4 grinds black pepper

For the seasoned tomatoes:

1 lb assorted cherry tomatoes—stems removed

1 tablespoon olive oil

1 teaspoon fig balsamic vinegar

Pinch coarse sea salt

3-4 grinds black pepper

To finish the dish:

6 oz goat cheese log—chilled and then sliced into 8 disks

⅓ cup pistachios—chopped

2 oz microgreens

1 In a large shallow bowl, grate the yellow heirloom tomatoes on a box grater using the largest holes. There should be approximately 2 cups of juicy pulp. Stir in the olive oil, lemon juice, salt and pepper.

2 Pour the juice through a coarse strainer into a medium measuring jug. Press down on the solids to extract as much juice as possible. Discard any pulp remaining in the strainer.

3 Place the cherry tomatoes in a medium bowl. Pour boiling water over them, let rest for 60 seconds and drain. Rinse with cold water. Peel the tomatoes and place them back in the bowl.

4 In a small bowl, whisk together the olive oil, fig balsamic vinegar, salt and pepper. Pour the vinaigrette over the peeled cherry tomatoes and toss them gently until fully coated and glistening.

5 To assemble the dish, place a goat cheese disk in the center of each plate. Sprinkle with the chopped pistachios.

6 Pour the tomato juice in a thin layer around the goat cheese disk to cover the bottom of the plate.

7 Place the microgreens on top of the goat cheese. Top the microgreens with the cherry tomatoes. Serve with a warm baguette or toasted olive bread to mop up any tomato juices.

Green Tomato, Green Fig, Goat Cheese and Mint Salad

During the summer months, the tables at the farmers markets are groaning with a plethora of tomatoes—huge, multi-colored heirloom varieties that are just so tempting, it's hard to resist them all. A few years ago, I came across some gorgeous chartreuse Green Zebra tomatoes. They are streaked with vertical stripes which turn from pale green to yellow as they ripen, and their flavor evolves from tart and tangy to sweet and zingy when the tomatoes are fully ripe. They are particularly good when eaten with figs. This has become one of my favorite summer salads.

Serves 8 people

For the vinaigrette:

3 tablespoons olive oil

Zest and juice of 1 lemon

Zest and juice of 1 lime

Pinch coarse sea salt

4–5 grinds black pepper

For the salad:

10–12 Green Zebra tomatoes—cut into eighths

10–12 green figs—quartered

1/2 cup fresh mint leaves

2 cups arugula

2 tablespoons finely chopped chives

3 stalks green onions—finely chopped

2 oz goat cheese—crumbled

1 In a medium salad bowl, whisk together all the vinaigrette ingredients to make an emulsion. Place salad utensils over the vinaigrette

2 Place all the salad ingredients in the bowl on top of the salad utensils. When ready to serve, toss the salad well, taking care not to smoosh the figs.

Club 55 Crudités Salad

Located halfway along the 5 kilometer stretch of white sand Pampelone beach on the Côte d'Azur, the iconic Club 55 is a bucolic, enchanted oasis that inspires languorous lunches. The restaurant's tables, clad in Provençale blue tablecloths, situated steps from the sand on a large terracotta terrace, are shaded by large, white canvas awnings. The food is fresh, local and simply prepared. Lunch often begins with huge *panier de crudités* served on a rustic cork tray—with many of the vegetables coming from the Club's own organic garden—accompanied by assorted vinaigrettes and aioli. Those magnificent *paniers* inspired this salad.

Serves 8 people

For the mustard vinaigrette:

1½ tablespoons Dijon
    mustard

¼ cup olive oil

1 tablespoon white wine
    vinegar

Pinch of salt

3-4 grinds black pepper

For the salad:

3 large or 6 medium red
    heirloom tomatoes—
    cored and cut into eighths

2 endives—ends trimmed,
    thinly sliced

1 large fennel—quartered
    lengthwise, thinly sliced

1 small bunch breakfast
    radishes—trimmed,
    thinly sliced

1 cup basil leaves—
    stacked, rolled tightly
    and thinly sliced

1 teaspoon chopped chives

1 tablespoon finely chopped
    flat-leaf parsley

3-4 white mushrooms—
    very thinly sliced

8 hardboiled eggs—
    peeled and quartered

1. In a large salad bowl, whisk together all the vinaigrette ingredients to make an emulsion. Place serving utensils over the vinaigrette.

2. Add all the salad ingredients, except the eggs, to the salad bowl. When ready to serve, toss the salad well. Divide among eight dinner plates and arrange the egg quarters on top.

Tarte aux Tomates

This is the dish to make when you find those huge, luscious heirloom tomatoes at the market, or if you are lucky enough to have a green thumb (I don't) and grow them yourself (I wish I could). The tart is savory, salty and juicy, and a lovely showcase for the beautiful toms.

Serves 8 people

For the pastry:

9 oz (2 cups) unbleached all-purpose flour

5½ oz (11 tablespoons) cold butter—chilled, cut into small pieces.

1 large egg

2 tablespoons finely chopped chives

Zest of 1 lemon

Pinch of salt

For the tomato filling:

2 tablespoons Dijon mustard

2 oz grated Gruyère, Compté or cheddar cheese

2 medium firm ripe yellow heirloom tomatoes—cored, thinly sliced horizontally

2 medium firm ripe red heirloom tomatoes—cored, thinly sliced horizontally

2 medium-sized firm ripe green heirloom tomatoes—cored, thinly sliced horizontally

1 tablespoon basil olive oil

Black pepper

Flake sea salt

1 Preheat the oven to 400 degrees.

2 Butter a 12-inch fluted tart pan with a removable bottom.

3 Place all the pastry ingredients in the bowl of a food processor fitted with a metal blade. Pulse until the mixture resembles coarse breadcrumbs. Use longer pulses until the dough forms a ball. Wrap the dough in plastic wrap and refrigerate for 20 minutes.

4 On a floured board, roll out the dough to a 14-inch circle. Line the tart pan with the dough. Trim the edges with a sharp knife and prick the dough with a fork. Line the dough with parchment paper and fill with pie weights or dried beans. Bake for 18-20 minutes until a pale golden color. Carefully remove the parchment paper and weights and bake for 5 more minutes. Remove from the oven and let cool for 5-10 minutes.

5 Spread the mustard over the bottom of the tart shell and sprinkle with the grated cheese.

6 Starting from the outside edge of the tart, arrange the tomato slices in alternating and overlapping concentric circles. Drizzle with olive oil. Grind some fresh pepper over the tomatoes—8-10 grinds should do the trick.

7 Bake in the center of the oven for 10 minutes or until the tomatoes are warmed though but not losing their shape or becoming watery. Sprinkle a little flake salt over the tart and serve while warm.

Roasted Black Cod with Olives, Pistachios and Saffron-Tomato Sauce

This is all about the sauce. It is sweet, savory and slightly piquant, and is complemented by the salty olives and pistachios that top the fish. I like to serve this with big slices of lightly toasted rustic olive bread to dip into the sauce.

Serves 8 people

For the sauce:

Olive oil

1 large yellow onion—peeled and diced

8 large tomatoes (approximately 2 lbs)

10–12 saffron threads

Salt

Black pepper

1 cup vegetable or chicken stock

2 tablespoons tomato paste

For the fish:

2$^{1}/_{2}$ lbs black cod

1 cup mixed olives—pitted and roughly chopped

$^{1}/_{2}$ cup pistachios—chopped

$^{1}/_{4}$ cup finely chopped flat-leaf parsley leaves

$^{1}/_{4}$ cup finely chopped chives

Zest and juice of 1 lemon

1. To make the sauce, heat a little olive oil in a large saucepan. Sauté the chopped onion until it is translucent and soft, about 8–10 minutes

2. In a medium shallow bowl, grate the tomatoes on the large holes of a box grater. Discard the skins.

3. Pour the tomato pulp and juice into the pan with the onions. Add the saffron and cook for 10 minutes. When the sauce has started to thicken and the tomatoes have lost most of their water, add a large pinch of salt and a few grinds of pepper. Stir in the stock and the tomato paste. Continue cooking over low heat until the sauce has thickened, about 15–20 minutes.

4. Preheat the oven to 325 degrees.

5. Pour a little olive oil into a baking pan that is large enough to hold the fish. Place the fish in the pan and turn it once or twice to coat with the oil.

6. In a small bowl, combine the olives, nuts, parsley, chives, lemon zest and lemon juice. Spoon the mixture on top of the black cod filets.

7. Bake in the center of the oven until completely opaque, about 18–20 minutes. Serve on warm plates surrounded by the saffron sauce.

NOTE: The sauce can be made up to 48-hours in advance and kept refrigerated until ready to use.

Tomato and Lentils du Puy Curry with Cucumber Raita

This curry is flavored with a mixture of curry seasoning and the North African spice mix, *ras el hanout*, as I love the extra depth they give to the tomatoes and lentils. The vegetables become so fragrant as they cook, that it smells divine in the kitchen. As a result, I often find myself sneaking a spoonful, or two, or three, before it's dinner time. This has become one of my favorite curries.

Serves 8 people

For the lentils:

1 cup lentils du Puy—rinsed

1 red onion—
     peeled and diced

1 carrot—peeled,
     cut into 4 pieces

5 cups water

Pinch of salt

4–5 grinds black pepper

For the curry:

Olive oil

2 large onions—
     peeled and sliced

1 large red onion—
     peeled and sliced

2 tablespoons curry powder

1 tablespoon *ras el hanout*

2 1/2 lbs Roma tomatoes—
     quartered and then
     puréed until smooth

1/2 cup golden raisins

2 lbs heirloom tomatoes
     (assorted varieties)—
     sliced

1/2 cup cilantro leaves

For the raita:

1 1/4 cups Greek yogurt

1 Persian cucumber—
     peeled and diced

2 tablespoons finely
     chopped chives

3 green onions—trimmed
     and thinly sliced

3 tablespoons olive oil

Large pinch of salt

Juice of 1 lemon

1   Place the lentils, red onion, carrot and cold water in a large saucepan over medium-high heat. Add the salt and pepper and bring to a boil. Reduce the heat and simmer until the lentils are barely tender, about 20 minutes. Drain through a mesh sieve and discard the carrots.

2   Pour 3 tablespoons olive oil into a large saucepan over medium heat. Add the onions and cook, stirring frequently, until softened and translucent, about 6–7 minutes. Stir in the curry powder and *ras el hanout* and continue cooking for 5 minutes.

3   Add the puréed tomatoes and golden raisins to the onions. Mix well and cook for 8–10 minutes, or until the tomato liquid has reduced by one-third.

4   Add the sliced tomatoes and cook for 15 minutes.

5   Gently stir in the lentils and cook for 5 minutes to warm through.

6   Put the raita ingredients into a small bowl and mix well.

7   To serve, spoon the curry into warmed bowls and spoon a dollop of the raita and cilantro leaves on top. I like to serve this with warmed naan bread.

Tomato and Lemon-Wrapped Roasted Halibut

During the summer months, I often have impromptu Sunday lunches in the garden with friends and family. These are relaxed, all afternoon affairs with lots of good food and laughter. I'll often run down to the harbor in the morning to see what fresh fish is available, and build the menu around that. This dish is great for a crowd as it multiplies easily, it's quick to prepare, and cooks in less than 30 minutes. I usually serve it with assorted salads or a black rice mixed with herbs.

Serves 8 people

Olive oil

2 large red onions—peeled, halved and thinly sliced

2 large yellow onions—peeled, halved and thinly sliced

Coarse sea salt

2 tablespoons *herbes de Provence*

2½ lbs halibut filet

2 or 3 large heirloom tomatoes—thinly sliced horizontally

3-4 lemons—thinly sliced

Salt

Black pepper

1 Preheat the oven to 350 degrees.

2 Pour a little olive oil into a large skillet over medium-high heat. Add the onions and a good pinch of sea salt and cook, stirring frequently, until soft, about 5-7 minutes. Stir in the *herbes de Provence* and continue to cook for 10 minutes. Remove from the heat and let cool for 10-15 minutes.

3 Spread the cooked onions in the bottom of a roasting pan. Place the halibut on top of the onions. Cover the fish with alternating rows of the tomato and lemon slices. Drizzle with a little olive oil and sprinkle with a good pinch of salt and a few grinds of fresh pepper.

4 Bake in the center of the oven for 20-22 minutes. Serve on warm plates.

ZUCCHINI & SQUASH

Zucchini Cappuccino

~

Roasted Acorn
Squash Salad with
Moroccan Spices

~

Roasted Zucchini
Terrine

~

Caramelized Onion Tart
with Zucchini Ribbons

~

Stuffed Delicata
Squash

~

Roasted Pattypan
Squash

~

Fusilli with Grilled
Zucchini and Pea
Tendril Pesto

~

Roasted Vegetable
"Risotto"

~

Zucchini and Goat
Cheese Soufflé

~

Zucchini, Spinach and
Cheese Clafoutis

Zucchini Cappuccino with Lime Crème Fraîche

Every now and then I come across a cooking utensil, a beautiful platter or a bowl that inspires me to make a particular dish. In this case, it was a set of whimsical coffee cups I found in one of my favorite stores. Porch, in the little seaside town of Carpinteria, is filled with unique and enchanting objects for the home and garden. Thank you to the charming owners, Diana and Christie, for these beautiful cups and the inspiration for this chilled soup!

Serves 8 people

Olive oil

2 large onions—peeled and finely chopped

7-8 medium-sized zucchini—ends trimmed, coarsely chopped

8 cups vegetable stock

Salt

Black pepper

2 cups shelled English peas

½ bunch flat-leaf parsley—finely chopped

½ cup heavy whipping cream

½ cup crème fraîche

Zest and juice of 1 lime

Small bunch of chives—finely chopped

1 Pour a little olive oil into a large saucepan over medium heat. Add the chopped onions and cook until lightly golden, about 3–4 minutes. Add the zucchini and cook, stirring frequently for 2–3 minutes. Add the vegetable stock, a good pinch of salt and 5-6 grinds of pepper, reduce the heat and simmer the vegetables for 20 minutes.

2 Stir in the English peas and parsley. Cook for 1 minute.

3 Use an immersion blender, food processor or blender to purée the soup until completely smooth. The soup should have a very light, almost frothy consistency.

4 Whisk the heavy cream in a medium bowl until it forms soft peaks.

5 In a small bowl, combine the crème fraîche, lime zest, juice and all but one tablespoon of the chives. Gently fold the mixture into the whipped cream.

6 Serve the soup in cups or small bowls with a spoonful of the crème fraîche "foam" and a light sprinkling of the reserved chives.

Roasted Acorn Squash Salad with Moroccan Spices

Tables piled high with pumpkins, butternut, delicata and acorn squash at the farmers market are a sure sign that autumn has arrived. It's at this time of year, when the weather can still be a bit balmy in Southern California, that I'll make salads with assorted squash, rather than soups or stews. This is a light dish that captures the flavors of the season.

Serves 8 people

For the acorn squash:

2 tablespoons olive oil

1 tablespoon *ras el hanout*

Large pinch coarse sea salt

2 acorn squash—peeled, halved, seeded, then cut into 1/3-inch slices

2/3 cup (4 oz) sprouted peanuts

For the yogurt vinaigrette:

1/4 cup Greek yogurt

1 tablespoon tahini

Juice and zest of 1 lemon

Zest of 1 lime

2 tablespoons olive oil

Black pepper

For the salad:

1/2 lb mixed salad greens

1/2 cup cilantro leaves

1/2 cup flat-leaf parsley leaves

2 tablespoons finely chopped chives

1 Preheat the oven to 400 degrees.

2 In a large bowl, whisk together 2 tablespoons olive oil, the *ras el hanout* and a good pinch of salt. Add the squash slices and toss to coat well.

3 Place the squash slices on an oiled baking sheet and roast for 15 minutes. Add the peanuts and roast for another 10–15 minutes. The squash should be tender if a knife can be easily inserted. Remove from the oven and let cool to room temperature.

4 While the squash is roasting, whisk together the yogurt, tahini, lemon zest and juice, lime zest and 2 tablespoon olive oil in a large salad bowl. Place serving utensils over the yogurt vinaigrette. Place the mixed greens and herbs on top of the utensils.

5 Toss the salad greens until well coated in the vinaigrette. Add the squash and toss gently. Serve warm.

Roasted Zucchini Terrine

This spectacular terrine is a labor of love, but it is oh so delicious!

Serves 8 to 10 people

Olive oil

2 lbs long zucchini—
   ends trimmed, peeled
   into thin strips

2 lbs long yellow squash—
   ends trimmed, peeled
   into thin strips

1/2 lb purple or green
   asparagus—woody
   ends trimmed

Olive oil

Salt

Black pepper

1/3 cup feta cheese

1/4 cup plain whole milk
   yogurt

1 tablespoon crème fraîche

1 tablespoon cream cheese

1 cup roughly chopped
   basil leaves

2 tablespoons roughly
   chopped parsley leaves

1 Preheat the oven to 350 degrees.

2 Line a 10-inch long terrine with plastic wrap so that the plastic drapes over the edges.

3 Drizzle a little olive oil onto two large rimmed sheet pans. Keeping the zucchini slices separated by color and in a single layer, bake the zucchini slices in batches. Sprinkle each batch with a pinch of salt and 4-5 grinds of pepper. Bake for 10 minutes. Set aside to cool.

4 Sauté the asparagus spears with a little olive oil in a large skillet over medium heat. Cook until *al dente* and lightly golden, about 3-4 minutes. Set aside to cool.

5 Combine the feta, yogurt, crème fraîche, cream cheese, basil and parsley in a beeker, deep narrow bowl or jar. (A mason jar works well, too.) Purée with an immersion blender until smooth. Leave at room temperature.

6 Line the bottom and sides of the terrine with the zucchini slices so that they extend over the sides by about 1 1/2 to 2 inches. To do this, lay two slices of the same color zucchini, end to end, across the terrine, slightly overlapping them in the base of the mold. Alternate between the yellow and green zucchini all the way along the mold.

7 To fill the terrine, cover the bottom with 2 layers of zucchini strips laid lengthwise. Spoon a little of the yogurt mixture over the zucchini strips, spreading it to cover the zucchini entirely. Repeat with 2 layers of yellow squash and the yogurt mixture.

8 Repeat step 7.

9 Next, add a layer of asparagus placing the stalks in alternating directions, lengthwise. Cover with more of the yogurt mixture. Add another double layer of green asparagus and the yogurt mixture. Finish filling the terrine with a double layer of yellow squash and the remaining yogurt mixture.

10 Fold the zucchini strips lining the terrine over the filling. Fold the plastic wrap over the top of the terrine. Place in the freezer for 30 minutes, then refrigerate until ready to serve.

11 To serve, peel back the plastic wrap and invert the terrine onto a cutting board. Remove the mold and the plastic wrap. Cut the terrine into 1/2-inch thick slices.

Caramelized Onion Tart with Zucchini Ribbons

Onion tarts are among my favorite Provençal dishes. This variation includes roasted shaved zucchini ribbons and goat cheese; I like to serve it with a peppery green salad.

Serves 8 to 10 people

For the filling:

Olive oil

3 large white onions—peeled, halved and finely sliced

3 torpedo or red onions—peeled, halved and finely sliced

Salt and black pepper

6 large zucchini—ends trimmed, shaved into thin ribbons

For the pastry:

9 oz (2 cups) unbleached all-purpose flour

5 oz butter—chilled, cut into small pieces

2 teaspoons olive oil

2 teaspoons lemon thyme leaves—finely chopped

1 large egg

Zest of 1 lemon

Pinch of salt

For the goat cheese:

5 oz slightly soft goat cheese—at room temperature

2 tablespoons finely chopped flat-leaf parsley

1 Pour a little olive oil into a large saucepan over medium heat. Add the onions, a large pinch of salt and 5–6 grinds of pepper; stir frequently and cook until the onions are completely soft and slightly golden. This will take at least 15 minutes. Set aside to cool.

2 Preheat the oven to 400 degrees.

3 Place the zucchini ribbons on a large rimmed sheet pan. Drizzle with a little olive oil, add a sprinkling of salt and pepper, and toss to coat. Roast the zucchini for 8–10 minutes. Remove from the oven and allow the zucchini to cool in the pan.

4 Butter an 11 or 12-inch fluted tart pan with a removable bottom.

5 Place all the dough ingredients into the bowl of a food processor, fitted with a metal blade. Pulse until the mixture resembles coarse breadcrumbs, then use longer pulses until the dough forms a ball. Wrap the dough in plastic wrap and refrigerate for 20 minutes.

6 Place the unwrapped dough on a lightly floured work surface. Roll out the dough to a 14-inch round, 1/4-inch thick. Line the tart pan with the dough, trim the edges with a sharp knife and prick the bottom with a fork.

7 Line the dough with a piece of parchment paper and fill the tart shell with pie weights or dried beans. Bake for 20 minutes. The crust should be a pale golden color.

8 Take the tart shell from the oven, remove the parchment paper and pie weights, and return the tart shell to the oven to bake for 5 more minutes. The shell should be golden brown. Remove from the oven and cool on a wire rack for 8–10 minutes.

9 Using a spoon, cream together the parsley and goat cheese. Gently spread the mixture on the bottom of the tart. Spoon the cooked onions onto the goat cheese and spread them to the edge. Heap the zucchini ribbons on top and then return the tart to the oven for 5 minutes. Serve while still warm.

Stuffed Delicata Squash

These beautiful golden squash have a sweet, delicate flavor, a creamy texture, and are entirely edible—yes, skin included. They are also the perfect receptacles for stuffing. In this version, they're packed with forbidden rice that's chock full of herbs and pistachios, and have a lively citrus zing.

Serves 8 people

For the squash:

8 small delicata squash—
  halved lengthwise,
  seeds removed

Olive oil

Salt

Black pepper

For the stuffing:

1 cup black rice—
  well rinsed

3 tablespoons finely
  chopped flat-leaf parsley

3 tablespoons finely
  chopped chives

2 tablespoons pistachios—
  finely chopped

2 green tomatoes—diced

Zest of 1 lime

Juice and zest of 1 lemon

2 tablespoons olive oil

Salt

Black pepper

1   Preheat the oven to 350 degrees.

2   Place the squash cut side up on a baking sheet. Drizzle with a little olive oil and sprinkle with a little salt and pepper. Roast for 30-35 minutes, or until a knife is easily inserted.

3   While the squash is roasting, prepare the stuffing. Place the rice in a small saucepan with $1\frac{1}{2}$ cups of water and a pinch of salt. Bring to a boil. Reduce heat to low. Cover and cook for 20-25 minutes, or until the rice is tender and the water has been absorbed.

4   Place the cooked rice and the remaining stuffing ingredients in a medium bowl and mix well to combine.

5   Fill the cooked squash with the stuffing mixture. Serve warm.

NOTE: This is lovely with a spoonful of yogurt or some crumbled goat cheese on top. I like to serve this with a green salad.

Roasted Pattypan Squash

Every week, one can find no less than six farmers markets in and around the city of Santa Barbara, including one on Tuesday afternoons along a stretch of State Street, the city's main thoroughfare. On a recent warm Tuesday evening, people ambled past stands, tasting plump berries, sampling fragrant olive oils and munching on sweet peaches. We were serenaded by an excellent young musician playing a tenor sax, and his classic, soul-satisfying jazz drifted through the crowd. It was the sort of evening that puts a smile on your face. There were mounds of summer fruit, huge bunches of fragrant herbs and a dazzling array of the summer's first crop of squash. I came upon these jewel-like pattypan squash and tiny zucchini. They were perfect and irresistible—a little like the jazz that evening.

Serves 8 people

3 lbs small pattypan squash

Olive oil

2 lemons—cut into eighths

5-6 shallots—peeled, quartered lengthwise

8-10 sprigs lemon thyme

Salt and black pepper

1/2 lb purple kale (baby leaves, if available)

1 cup fresh basil leaves (mixed varieties, if available)

1 cup assorted Provençal olives—pitted

Goat cheese (crumbled), Manchego or Gruyère (grated)—optional

1 Preheat the oven to 375 degrees.

2 Place the pattypan squash into a roasting pan. Squeeze juice from the lemon wedges and add them to the pan. Add the shallots and thyme. Drizzle with a little olive oil and sprinkle with salt and pepper. Roast for 25 minutes.

3 Remove the pan from the oven and mix in the kale leaves. Return the pan to the oven and roast the vegetables for an additional 10 minutes.

4 In a large bowl, combine the roasted vegetables and their pan juices with the olives and basil leaves. Toss well and taste for seasoning. Add a little fresh lemon juice for brightness. Serve on individual plates and top with a little cheese.

Fusilli with Grilled Zucchini and Pea Tendril Pesto

My daughter has a penchant for pesto. I recently made a bright green batch of classic pesto that I spread on crostini with goat cheese. Olivia found it completely irresistible and polished off the entire platter before my dinner guests arrived. "Oops! Sorry, Mum," she said as she walked out of the kitchen with a green blob of pesto in the corner of her mouth and a cheeky smile on her face. Now, out of basil, I decided to make a different pesto using pea greens, the long tendrils that grow on pea vines. These greens make a vibrant, slightly spicy pesto that's fresh, invigorating, and perfect for spring. This pasta dish is quick to make; the veggies can be grilled, roasted or sautéed with a touch of olive oil, and you can add spring peas and asparagus to it for a seasonal variation. This is also wonderful for a picnic as it's delicious at any temperature.

Serves 8 people as a first course or 4 as a main course

For the pesto:

1/2 cup olive oil

Zest and juice of 1 large
    or 2 small lemons

6 oz pea tendrils—
    roughly chopped

2 oz feta cheese

Salt

Black pepper

For the pasta:

Olive oil

1 lb fusilli

1 tablespoon butter

Salt

Black pepper

For the vegetables:

3 zucchini—ends trimmed,
    cut on a bias into 1/4-inch
    ovals

3 yellow squash—ends
    trimmed, cut on a bias
    into 1/4-inch ovals

8 spring onions—
    ends trimmed, cut
    into 1-inch pieces

Salt and black pepper

Romano cheese—
    for grating

1   Using a blender or food processor, blend the olive oil, lemon juice and the pea tendrils to make a thick pesto. Add the feta, a pinch of salt and some pepper, scrape down the sides and blend again. Let rest at room temperature while you prepare the pasta and vegetables.

2   Bring a large pot of salted water to a boil. Add the pasta and cook until *al dente*, approximately 10 minutes. Drain the pasta and return it to the pot. Add the butter, a good pinch of salt and 5–6 grinds of pepper. Toss well.

3   Preheat a grill pan over medium-high heat.

4   Pour a little olive oil into a large bowl. Add the sliced vegetables, a good pinch of salt and some pepper and toss to coat well. Grill the vegetables in batches for 2 minutes on each side. Be careful not to overcook them. Add the grilled vegetables to the pasta.

5   Pour the pesto over the pasta and grilled vegetables and mix carefully to keep the zucchini slices intact. Serve in warmed bowls, with shaved or grated Romano cheese.

Roasted Vegetable "Risotto"

Please don't groan when you see the list of ingredients for this recipe. It may be long, but the prep work is just chopping and stirring—well, maybe a fair amount of chopping—but the end result will produce a "risotto" bathed in a fragrant golden stock that exudes the essence of summer in every morsel.

Serves 8 people

For the saffron stock:

Olive oil

1 leek—trimmed, rinsed clean, roughly chopped

1 onion—peeled, and diced

3 carrots—peeled and sliced

2 stalks celery—chopped

3 1/2 cups cold water

6-8 threads of saffron

1/4 teaspoon turmeric

For the risotto:

Olive oil

1 butternut squash—peeled and cut into small dice

1-2 golden beets—peeled and cut into small dice

8 large carrots (different colors)—peeled and cut into small dice

1 tablespoon vegetable herb mix or *herbes de Provence*

Salt

Black pepper

4 zucchini—cut into small dice

3-4 small yellow squash— cut into small dice

2 onions—peeled and cut into small dice

1 leek—trimmed, rinsed, white and light green parts diced

3 shallots—peeled and diced

1/2 cup white wine

3 cups saffron stock

1/2 bunch chives— finely chopped

1. To make the stock, heat a little olive oil into a medium saucepan. Sauté the vegetables for 5 minutes, stirring frequently. Add the water, saffron and turmeric. Simmer for 15 minutes. Remove from the heat until ready to use. Then strain and discard the vegetables.

2. Preheat the oven to 400 degrees.

3. Pour a little olive onto a rimmed sheet pan and add the butternut squash, beets, carrots and herb mix. Shake the pan so that all the vegetables are well coated. Sprinkle with salt and pepper and roast for 10 minutes.

4. Add the chopped zucchini and squash to the pan with the root vegetables, and roast for 20 minutes, stirring the vegetables once or twice.

5. While the vegetables are roasting, heat a little olive oil in a large saucepan or dutch oven over medium heat. Sauté the onions, leek and shallots until they are soft and translucent, about 10 minutes. Add the wine and cook until it has completely evaporated. Add 1 cup of the saffron broth and simmer for 10 minutes.

6. Add the roasted vegetables to the saucepan with the onions and stock. Add the remaining saffron stock, bring the heat back up to medium and cook for 3 minutes.

7. Serve the risotto on warmed plates or in shallow bowls. Spoon some of the stock over the vegetables.

Zucchini and Goat Cheese Soufflé

I know a lot of people who point-blank refuse to make a soufflé, claiming that it's too difficult, too risky, too nerve-wracking. I promise you that making soufflés is none of these things. From a few simple ingredients—butter, flour, milk and eggs—you can create an ethereal dish in less than one hour that will draw appreciative oohs and aahs from your dinner guests. It is part alchemy, part heat, and a careful folding in of egg whites that create a magnificent soufflé. Watching it rise as it bakes is part of the excitement, but the best moment, for me—other than eating it, of course—is when I take the golden topped creation out of the oven. It makes me smile every time.

Serves 8 people

For the vegetables:

Olive oil

3 shallots—peeled and thinly sliced

1 teaspoon *herbes de Provence*

3 medium zucchini—quartered lengthwise and thinly sliced

Salt

Black pepper

2 tablespoon finely chopped chives

For the soufflé:

4 tablespoons butter

3 tablespoons unbleached flour

1⅓ cups milk

2 tablespoons crème fraîche

6 oz goat cheese

5 egg yolks

8 egg whites

1 Heat a little olive oil in a medium saucepan. Sauté the shallots with the *herbes de Provence* for 3–4 minutes until a pale golden color. Add the zucchini, a pinch of salt, 6–7 grinds of pepper and cook, stirring frequently, until browned, approximately 10 minutes. Mix in the chives and remove from the heat.

2 Preheat the oven to 400 degrees.

3 Generously butter the inside of a 2-quart soufflé dish using 1 tablespoon of butter.

4 Melt the remaining 3 tablespoons of butter in a large saucepan over low heat. Stir in the flour and cook until it has completely absorbed the butter and thickens into a paste, 2–3 minutes. Slowly pour in the milk, whisking continuously until the mixture thickens. Remove from the heat.

5 Add the crème fraîche, cooked zucchini and cheese, stirring well to combine. When the mixture has cooled a bit, whisk in the egg yolks one at a time, stirring continuously until the mixture is smooth and homogenous.

6 Beat the egg whites until stiff peaks form, however, do not overbeat them as this will create a dry soufflé. Gently fold the egg whites into the soufflé base until they are completely incorporated—there should be no pockets of egg whites. Gently pour the mixture into the prepared soufflé dish.

7 Bake for 40 minutes. Serve immediately.

Zucchini, Spinach and Cheese Clafoutis

Clafoutis are, traditionally, cherry-filled baked flans. This is a savory version, packed with oodles of vegetables and mounds of cheese. It's a perfect brunch or lunchtime dish.

Serves 8 people as a first course or 4 people as a main course

3 cups milk

1 tablespoon chives

1 tablespoon dill

3 oz (2/3 cup) unbleached all-purpose flour

5 large eggs

4 oz cheddar cheese— grated

2 tablespoons crème fraîche

Olive oil

1 large onion—peeled and chopped

1 small bunch green onions— ends trimmed, white and light green parts chopped

1 yellow squash—chopped into 1/2-inch pieces

1 green zucchini—chopped into 1/2-inch pieces

Salt

Black pepper

2 cups packed baby spinach leaves

1 Preheat the oven to 400 degrees.

2 In a medium saucepan, warm the milk with the chives and dill for 4–5 minutes over low heat. Remove the pan from the heat.

3 Place the flour in a large bowl. Whisk in one egg at a time. The batter should be completely smooth. Slowly pour in the milk mixture and whisk until the batter is free of any lumps. Add three-quarters of the cheese, the crème fraîche, a good pinch of salt and 7–8 grinds of pepper and mix until smooth. The batter will be thin.

4 Pour a little olive oil into a large cast iron pan or ovenproof skillet set over medium-high heat. Sauté the onions and green onions until completely soft and golden, about 8–10 minutes. Add the zucchini and cook until golden brown, 7–10 minutes. Add the spinach and cook until wilted.

5 Pour the batter over the vegetables. Place in the center of the oven and bake for 10 minutes. Scatter the remaining cheese over the top and continue baking for 20 minutes. The clafoutis is done when the custard is just set. The top should be golden brown. Serve at room temperature.

Suppliers & Sources

I am often asked where I buy my produce, fish, meat, flowers and wine. These purveyors, shops and markets are the ones I use whilst in California. They have all proven to be reliable, and I heartily recommend them.

SANTA BARBARA

CHEESE

C'est Cheese
www.cestcheese.com
(805) 965-0318

The best local shop for exquisite cheeses and gourmet items, run by the charming Kathryn and Michael Graham.

HERBS AND SPICES

Pascale's Kitchen
www.pascaleskitchen.com
(805) 965-5112

A great resource for exotic salts, herbs, spice blends and olive oils, and beautiful kitchen items.

PATISSERIE

Renaud's Patisserie and Bistro
www.renaudsbakery.com
(805) 569-2400

There are croissants, and then there are Renaud's croissants—truly some of the best-tasting confections and macarons in California.

PRODUCE

Santa Barbara's Farmers Market
www.sbfarmersmarket.org
(805) 962-5354

At the market, I would highly recommend the following farms:

BD's Earthtrine Farms
(805) 640-1423

Fragrant herbs and wonderful vegetables.

Fat Uncle Farms
www.fatunclefarms.com

They have THE most incredible blistered almonds.

Ojai Valley Sprouts
Source of the most beautiful microgreens

Peacock Farms
www.peacockfamilyfarms.com

Superb eggs and dried fruit.

Pudwill Farms
(805) 268-4536

Great berries and figs.

Roots Organic Farm
Spectacular vegetables from Jacob Grant abound at this stand.

The Garden of .....
For the most beautiful and flavorful lettuce, herbs, leeks and tomatoes.

Mesa Produce
(805) 962-1645

This store is an excellent source for locally-farmed organic produce.

SEAFOOD

Santa Barbara Fish Market
www.sbfish.com
(805) 965-9564

Excellent local market at the harbor where you can buy fresh fish that have come right off the local boats.

WINERIES

Santa Barbara County is home to many wonderful wineries that produce world-class vintages. Here are some of my favorites:

Alma Rosa Winery
www.almarosawinery.com

Buttonwood Farm and Winery
www.buttonwoodwinery.com

Casa Dumetz
www.casadumetzwines.com
(805) 344-1900

Riverbench Winery
www.riverbench.com

Zaca Mesa Winery
www.zacamesa.com

LOS ANGELES

BREAD

La Brea Bakery
www.labreabakery.com
(323) 939-6813

America's most widely recognized artisan bakery sells delicious loaves from its original La Brea Blvd. location.

Gjusta
www.gjusta.com
(310) 314-0320

Opened in 2014 to acclaimed reviews, this bakery/hip Venice deli produces extraordinary crunchy luscious bread.

CHEESE

The Cheese Store
www.cheesestorebh.com
(310) 278-2855

The best cheese shop in Los Angeles, with more than 400 fabulous cheeses and other delicious culinary products.

GOURMET FOODS

Monsieur Marcel
www.mrmarcel.com
(323) 939-7792

Wonderful array of gourmet foods and cheese from France with an incredible selection of mustards, oils and vinegars.

PRODUCE & FLOWERS

Santa Monica's Wednesday Farmers Market
www.santa-monica.org/farmers_market

The now-famous market is one of the largest in California. This huge, diverse market supplies many of Los Angeles's great restaurants. It's worth a trip just to explore all sorts of seasonal goodies.

One of my favorite vendors there is **Windrose Farms**
www.windrosefarm.org

Fragrant heirloom tomatoes, squash, heirloom spuds and wonderful apples.

SEAFOOD

Santa Monica Seafood
www.smseafoodmarket.com
(310) 393-5244

A wonderful seafood store that supplies many of the top restaurants in Southern California. Their retail outlet is spectacular.

Weights & Measures

I am a firm believer in using a kitchen scale for baking. However, if you don't have a kitchen scale this chart should be helpful. It is a quick reference for volume, ounce, and gram equivalencies for common ingredients.

DRY MEASURES:	VOLUME	OUNCES	GRAMS
Unbleached all-purpose flour	1 cup	4 1/2	120
Granulated sugar	1 cup	7	198
Brown sugar (packed)	1 cup	7 1/2	213
Almond meal/flour	1 cup	3 3/8	95
Powdered sugar	1 cup	4	125

LIQUID MEASURES:	VOLUME	OUNCES	MILLILITERS
Water	1 cup	8	237
Cream	1 cup	8	237
Honey	1 cup	12	340
Olive oil	1/4 cup	2	60

WET MEASURES:	VOLUME	OUNCES	GRAMS
Butter	1/2 cup	4	117
Yogurt	1 cup	8	225

OVEN TEMPERATURES:

Fahrenheit	Celsius
32 degrees F *(freezing)*	0 degrees C *(freezing)*
200 degrees F *(water boils at 212°F)*	93 degrees C *(water boils at 100°C)*
250 degrees F	121 degrees C
300 degrees F	149 degrees C
350 degrees F	177 degrees C
400 degrees F	205 degrees C
450 degrees F	232 degrees C

NOTE:
Nearly all ovens outside the U.S. are calibrated in Celsius rather than Fahrenheit.

Index

Index

Index

Acknowledgments

This beautiful book came about with the help of a marvelous team of multi-talented and creative people.

I would like to thank all the extraordinary farmers whose produce appears on these pages: Jacob Grant from Roots Organic Farm; B.D (Robert Dautch) from Earthrine Farms; everyone at The Garden of ....., Ojai Valley Sprouts and Tutti Frutti Farms; and Mr. Her from Laos. I am in awe of your green thumbs. Every week, whatever the weather, you arrive at the farmers market and pile your tables high with the fruits (and vegetables) of your labor. Your food is not only beautiful but soul satisfying. So much of the inspiration for my writing, cooking, and the recipes in this book comes from walking through the market and seeing the delicious food you have grown. You nourish my creativity. Thank you for your incredibly hard work in making our food landscape a more wholesome one.

To Diana Dolan and Christy Boyd at Porch: Thank you for your gorgeous tableware that helped create beautiful backdrops for so many of our photos.

To the ultra-creative Mike Verbois: WOW—our eighth book together! Thank you for patiently and meticulously shooting this book (and the videos) over a nine-month period as each vegetable came into season. Once again, everything went seamlessly. Your exquisite attention to detail is reflected in every stunning photograph. I am, as always, extraordinarily grateful for your energy, your patience and your art. *Merci* Mike!

To Judi Muller: With this book, you have designed more than 1,000 pages of my cookbooks and every one is beautiful. Thank you for your discerning eye, elegant graphic design, and most of all, thank you for making our collaboration such an enjoyable one. I look forward to many more in the future.

To Ruth Verbois: Thank you for handling the myriad details of getting this, and all my books, out the door and into the hands of our booksellers and book buyers. You always handle so many details with aplomb. Thank you for helping make the first two books in this series—*Salade* and *Les Fruits*—such successes; I look forward to our continued adventures with *Les Légumes*.

To Susan Noble: A massive thank you for all you do and for *all* your efforts on my behalf. These books would not be here without you and the entire publishing group at M27 Editions.

To Shukri Farhad: What an incredible journey we have been on through the production, printing, publishing and promotion of my books. Thank you for your unwavering belief in me and my work, and for championing my endeavors. Thank you, too, to Tracy for leading the cheering section and encouraging every road trip and promotional event we have taken. I could not do this without the limitless support of you both. *Merci!*

To Sherry Mannello: I am once again at a loss for words... Your help in the kitchen and behind the scenes, enthusiasm, positive energy and devotion to this, and all my projects, is extraordinary. I am truly humbled by your efforts on my behalf over the past eight years. Thank you is just not enough!

To Nancy Whetter: You are quite remarkable! A huge thank you for all your support, interest, enthusiasm and encouragement; for tasting so many of the dishes; for your keen grammatical and editing sense; for your help promoting my books and for joining me on long book signing road trips. (Yes, more to come!) *Merci, merci mon amie.*

To Harriet Eckstein: Thank you for your editing assistance and especially for understanding my sometimes-peculiar phraseology and idiosyncratic British expressions, and for gently wrestling said verbiage into less convoluted text. Your constant encouragement, moral support and willingness to try all my concoctions is fabulous! You have gone above and beyond my friend, and I am so utterly grateful for all you do. *Merci à toi aussi mon amie.*

This has been a big project and one which unavoidably impacted those around me. To my children, Olivia and Alexandre, once again you have endured the daily photo shoots, the invasion of camera equipment and props throughout the house, and my endless recipe testing—although hopefully you enjoyed that part! I hugely appreciate your patience with all my ventures and peregrinations. I treasure you both more than you could ever know. *Merci mes enfants.*

To my parents: It is you who provided the foundation for my culinary passions, having instilled in me a desire to learn, to be curious, to taste and to create. You have given me your unconditional love, energy and support. I am, and always will be, eternally grateful. My books would not be here without you. *Encore, encore, mille fois merci.*